You Are So You!

The Path to Uplifting Hearts

Shirley Moore

an imprint of Skywater Holdings, LLC.

You Are So You!
The Path to Uplifting Hearts
Shirley Moore

First Published 2013 by Moore Ideas,
an imprint of Skywater Holdings, LLC.
www.MooreIdeas.com

Copyright © 2013 Shirley Moore.

All rights reserved. No part of this book may be used or reproduced, stored in a retrieval system, or transmitted in any form or by any means, electronic, mechanical, photocopying, recording, or otherwise, without the prior written permission of the copyright holder, except in the case of brief quotations in critical articles or reviews.

Cover art: Saundra E. Beretta - ***www.SaundraBerettaArt.com***   © S.E. BERETTA

ISBN: 978-0-615-85342-0
Library of Congress Control Number: 2013913621

Printed in the United States

10 9 8 7 6 5 4 3 2 1

Dedicated with love to my husband, John, whose Intangible Gifts of Joy and Laughter always find their smiling way to the inner spaces of my Heart.

Table of Contents

2 .... *Intangible Gifts From the Heart*

8 .... *Prepare Your Heart*

10 .... *Follow Your Heart*

14 .... *Open Your Heart* - **Say "Hello" With Your Eyes**

28 .... *Reveal Your Heart* - **Fond**

38 .... *Believing Heart* - **Turning Green** (Not an environmental statement)

50 .... *Adoring Heart* - **I'd Do Anything for "Good Boy"**

64 .... *Heart Memories* - **Remembering Kinda Gal**

74 .... *Connect Your Heart* - **Calling in Cold**

84 .... *Align Your Heart* - **Nowhere to go. Nothing to do.**

96 .... *Resilient Heart* - **Will They Have Avocados?**

106 .... *Expand Your Heart* - **My Cells Are Ringing**

116 .... *Receptive Heart* - **All Ears**

126 .... *Bold Heart* - **Six Bucks and a Kiss on the Cheek**

138 .... *Guiding Heart* - **Watch Your Hair, Lady**

150 .... *Heart Prism*

158 .... *Acknowledgments*

Time appears to unravel in her presence. As she directs her gaze into the future, words jostle for position and fragments of yet to be conversations float by. Her voice quivers, then gains momentum, layering her predictions with imagination. She examines her cards and speaks:

"I see a trip across a vast prairie. A mysterious woman stands on a mountaintop, wrapped in a blue silk robe. There is an incident… with a fountain pen."

One of my fondest childhood memories is of sitting on my grandmother's bed while she laid out her fortune cards and read my future. The one consistency in these always entertaining revelations, was that I would write a book. There have been a handful of times in the years since my grandmother's readings, that additional opportunities, emanating from a variety of cultures and spiritual backgrounds, have presented themselves as a vision and a version of what my future might hold. Again, the one thing they all have seemed certain of, was that I would write a book.

Despite the fact that I do not think of myself as a superstitious person, I do pay attention to patterns that emerge in my life. As a result of these predictions, I have attempted to keep journals of experiences that have had an impact on my life, relationships that have had a positive influence and ideas that have inspired me. I have kept scraps of paper, post its, notations in margins and all manner of thoughts in dismembered arrays. As the years have gone by, a reoccurring goal has been to find a format that would accommodate and connect these seemingly unrelated notations. At long last, a flash of insight has illuminated a way for me to accomplish what has become a self-fulfilling prophecy. As foretold, I have written a book, the title of which is, *You Are So You!* The Path to Uplifting Hearts.

Like all creative endeavors, this book has taken on a life of its own and I have become the vehicle of its expression.

I invite you to step over the threshold of gratitude, through the entryway of praise and into a treasure house filled with *Intangible Gifts*, where you will rehearse ways to show others the best versions of themselves. Your efforts will uplift people's hearts, elevate their moods and build Connections, by revealing the positive traits and talents that they possess.

Please allow this book to be your muse.

Follow *You Are So You!* The Path to Uplifting Hearts, as it illuminates the way to creating a Heart space of meaningful Connections.

Begin connecting to who you are by raising the vibrations of your own One on One Connections. Act from your Heart and you will discover more about why,

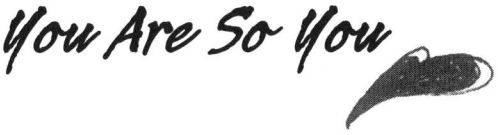

Intangible Gifts From the Heart

We all are curious about how others distinguish the essence of who we are.

We listen carefully to what might be exceptional, unique or inspirational about us.
We seek to understand the Connections we share.
These observations are important, because the perceptions of others color how we see ourselves and can inspire us to become the best versions of who we are.

Ask Yourself,
Who are the loved ones who have given meaning to your life,
The people who have made an impact upon you,
The mentors who have influenced your attitudes and behaviors,
The role models who have energized and inspired you,
The friends who have supported and encouraged you,
The souls who have made your life more joyful?

Big Zero

It was the day I became one big smile!

You know that feeling, the warm rush of delight that engulfs you and illuminates your Heart, as well as your face.

It was a milestone birthday for me and everyone brought *Intangible Gifts* to the celebration.

Traits for which I had hoped and strived to be acknowledged and appreciated were precisely identified and unwrapped. Qualities that I thought no one had noticed, but were important areas of growth for me, were displayed. The best version of myself, the essence of the person I believed I could become, came clearly into focus. All of these *Intangible Gifts* were part of such a heartfelt offering, that I was left feeling cherished and valued.

When someone reveals your *Intangible Gifts*, the qualities they respect, admire and adore, you will find yourself sighing a soft smile. What shines through is the best of who you are.

I frequently recall in detail the *Intangible Gifts* that people gave. This memory instantly boosts my spirits, raises my vibration, realigns my mood, and takes me to my happy place.

These *Intangible Gifts* are now a part of how I view myself. If, on occasion, I doubt my abilities, or get a bit lost in my shadow side, I can still find the person I aspire to be by viewing myself through the appreciative lens of my friends' eyes.

Was I the center of attention?
Absolutely!

Did I feel a little embarrassed receiving so many *Intangible Gifts* at once?
Yes.

Did I cherish every second?
Definitely!

When time blurs and my mind begins to think randomly and out of sequence, I believe that what will remain about that experience is an enduring bond that links us and a dreaming image of their smiles imprinted on my heart.

I have found such delight in giving my own *Intangible Gifts*, that it is has become the approach I use to express what others mean to me. The result is an amazing feeling of Connection to the people whose lives have woven in and out of my personal history. It is my wish that you too will discover a similar bond of belonging, because giving *Intangible Gifts* is one of the most persuasive ways in which we can cultivate meaningful Connections and add to the happiness of others.

Imagine the smiles you will bring forth, the Hearts you will lift, the moods you will elevate and the Connections you will deepen, when you turn your positive thoughts into positive energy by offering your most Heartfelt feelings as an *Intangible Gift*.

Giving and receiving *Intangible Gifts* is the way each of us can have a positive influence on how our personal worlds unfurl. We do this by expressing what we value and acknowledging who and what has influenced our growth. Giving life to the invisible and the intangible can be considered magic, your magic. Repairing the world is a daunting task, but each of us can aspire to create uplifting vibrations by offering *Intangible Gifts*.

When you present an *Intangible Gift*, attend to how it is delivered and with what intention and emotion it is given.

Wrap your Intangible Gifts extravagantly and tie them with ribbons and bows. Wrap them in brown paper and bundle them with string.

It doesn't matter as long as you are genuine.

It may be the thought that counts, but no one will know unless you make a *Place in Your Heart* for each person by revealing the *Intangible Gifts* they possess.

Don't be surprised if you find that exchanging Intangible Gifts transforms your world and the world of those you care about.

"I am giving you a Piece of My Mind."

What would your reaction be if you received this handwritten message from a friend?

Sometimes *Intangible Gifts* come disguised in a way that alters your preconceived ideas.

To my delight I discovered that she had indeed given me *a Piece of Her Mind* by sharing her private thoughts from a page in her journal. This unexpected, but very personal *Intangible Gift*, demonstrated how much she trusted in our friendship and cemented our Connection across the miles.

Tucked inside the pages of this book, you will encounter various *Pieces of My Mind*. You will recognize these *Pieces* as a compilation of indelible impressions others have left behind as profound influences on my life.

Often appearing as a maze of cherished stories, gentle musings and flashes of creativity, these memories eventually transform themselves into insights and life lessons learned. People from my present and my past wander around at will, and their wisdom seems to magically appear at the precise moment that it is most beneficial.

These relationships, some brief encounters, others long lived, have found their *Place in My Heart* and are now an integral part of my personal terrain. They are like familiar landmarks and their grace follows along wherever I go.

If you are the kind of person who loves to learn about new ways of seeing, thinking and being, I invite you to explore this world and its inner workings. By doing so, I hope that you will hear the affirming voices of your own relationships and experience the exuberant gestures that recognizing your *Intangible Gifts* and acknowledging the *Intangible Gifts* of others can produce.

Act from your Heart!

I have made space for you in this process, so that you too can present *Pieces of Your Mind* to the people you admire and appreciate. When we share our most Heartfelt thoughts, it is like giving others a *Piece of Our Mind* and a *Place in Our Heart*.

It is an Intangible Gift.

I refer to this kind of Intangible Gifting as a Heart Message.

Permit curiosity to direct you along the pathways leading to the *Places in Your Heart*. Go in search of the people who reside there, what they mean to you, why they are an enduring influence, and how their words and actions impact the way in which your personal essence unfolds each day.

This book is designed to support you as you discover various ways in which you can intensify the Connections with the people who dwell in your Heart. Giving and receiving *Intangible Gifts* is one of the most compelling ways in which we can create true Connections.

Invisible ties can seem rare, but they are worth striving for, because these Connections are what hold us all together and are an important dimension of our own happiness and well being.

The following pages will present you with inexhaustible opportunities to practice giving and receiving a very special *Intangible Gift,* the **Heart Message**.

What if you allowed your impressions to combine into insights and these insights to appear as messages from your Heart, a **Heart Message**?

Creating **Heart Messages** is a process, as well as a lifestyle choice.

It requires practice, intention, and effort.

Our reward is the opportunity to shape our own lives,
as well as the lives of others, by uplifting Hearts,
one message at a time.

"A gift is pure when it is given from the heart
to the right person at the right time
and at the right place,
and when we expect nothing in return."

Bhagavad Gita

Prepare Your Heart

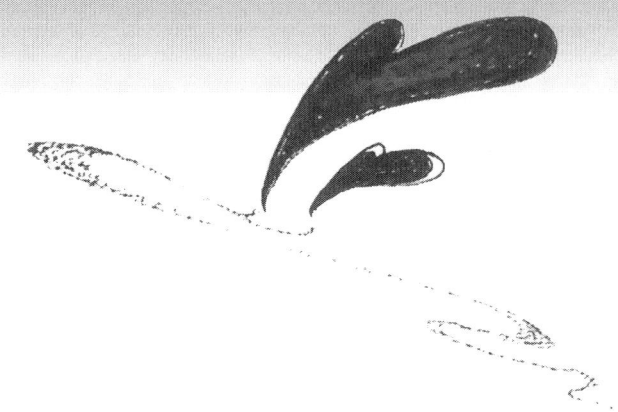

Prepare Your Heart to:

Identify the people who have made a lasting difference in your own life.

Spotlight the qualities that you admire in those who have played a role in your wellbeing.

Reflect on those who have expanded your beliefs, altered your perspectives, and opened your Heart.

Engage in a pattern of Connection that expresses your feelings for the ways in which people have enriched your life experiences.

Share your feedback on what you value in others, the impressions they have made and the images they project.

What kind of Heart do you have?

Is it open and eager to discover all it can become? When it is revealed, who gets to look inside? Does it believe in helping others shine? Does it speak in the language of love? Does it recall who left indelible marks? How does it connect the dots? Is its spirit aligned? Has its resilience been tested? Does it constantly expand and evolve? Is it receptive to the voices between the lines? Can it be bold? Will it glow rather than glare?

We are aware that we exhibit a wide range of emotions and we know what it feels like to experience fluctuations in our moods. We realize that we enjoy various kinds of intelligence, and we also resolve to develop strength, flexibility and stamina for our wellbeing.

But have you ever contemplated the various kinds of Hearts you possess?

Prepare Your Heart is the first in a **Collection of Heart Intentions** that you will discover as you continue exploring this book. Each subsequent chapter introduces you to a repertoire of **Heart Intentions** that will offer you unique ways of fostering meaningful Connections.

Can you prepare for every eventuality?
Unlikely.

Life is full of unanticipated happenings, some delightful and some challenging.
But you can *Prepare Your Heart* to enrich each day by selecting the most appropriate **Heart Intention** for any given situation.

Just being aware that it is possible to *Prepare Your Heart* is important to note.

Prepare Your Heart by choosing a **Heart Intention** that reflects the type of approach your Heart will take.

Prepare Your Heart to set the most positive tone available in that moment.

Pay attention to the kind of reaction you receive when you experiment with the various **Heart Intentions**. Which ones meet or exceed your expectations? If you find that you are struggling in a relationship, try a different **Heart Intention** and see what happens.

Follow Your Heart

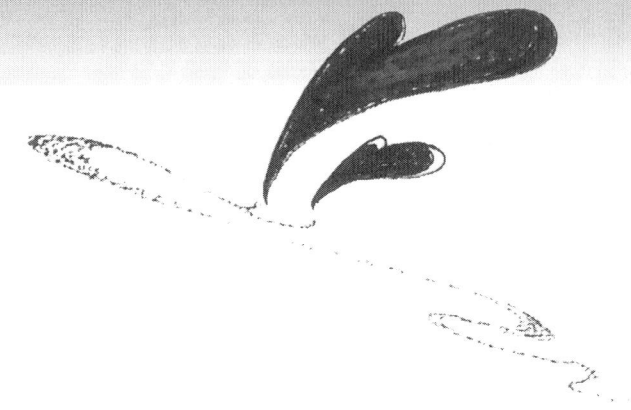

When you delve into your personal store of experiences, do you ever find
that there are wandering thoughts that you have long held close to your Heart?

What happens when you follow them?

Do you ever wish you knew more ways to bring out
the best in those with whom you come into contact?

Do you ever ask for insights into how to articulate to loved ones, to friends, colleagues,
even strangers in the grocery line, what your positive impressions are of them?

Do you consider how others have inspired you?

Do you wonder how best to lift your own spirits
or who to turn to as you seek fulfillment?

Follow Your Heart to Discover What Awaits You

Please consider the contents of this book to be your companion and your guide. Think of the chapters as places to enjoy and explore. Choose what speaks to you in the moment and allow yourself time to savor, to experience and to integrate the information. Play with the various **Heart Intentions**. Enjoy giving and receiving *Intangible Gifts*. Practice sharing **Heart Messages**. Develop a style that comes naturally to you. Listen to the voices within these pages, but listen most carefully to your own inner voice.

Within each chapter you will find the following format will consistently appear throughout the book.

Heart Intentions

You will be introduced to twelve **Heart Intentions**, inventive insights that demonstrate the impact intentions can have on the ways in which Connections are built and relationships unfold. A Heart title page will signal the opening of each section. The **Heart Intentions** you select will influence the way in which others will relate to you. Experiment with these **Heart Intentions** to determine which approaches will create the Connections you are seeking. This is how you Act from your Heart.

Intangible Gifts

Interspersed throughout each chapter is an array of *Intangible Gifts* that you may wish to bestow upon yourself or others. You may recognize these Gifts as traits you admire, qualities you respect, behaviors that please you, actions that support you, and wisdom that inspires or motives you. Be on the look out for the *Intangible Gifts* you wish to give or receive. Notice the *Intangible Gifts* that are already in your possession. Be generous. This kind of Gifting does not require a special occasion or a cash reserve, but it will cause people to celebrate!

Each chapter will concentrate upon an *Intangible Gift* for you to avail yourself of in improving your Connections to others.

Heart Companion to *Bring Along*

At the beginning of each chapter, you will be asked to *Bring Along* a certain *Intangible Gift* that you already possess. This gift is your **Heart Companion**. Use these *Bring Alongs* to build Connections. Each chapter will introduce you to a new *Bring Along* companion. (Example: your smile, your attention). *Bring Along* this companion in the form of your own self-awareness and make it a focal point of how you perceive the world. These **Heart Companions** are always there for you. They are willing to accompany you on every journey and they will help to set the tone for what ensues. They love to have a good time. You just have to remember to *Bring Them Along*.

Heart Tales

These are affirming and inspirational **Tales** that illustrate the power of using **Heart Intentions** and *Intangible Gifts* to enhance your relationships and strengthen your Connections. They are little *Pieces of My Mind*. I hope they will stir an emotion within your Heart, because this is not just a book to be read. It will require interaction and conscious thought, in order for the messages it speaks to relate to your life.

Heartfelt Connections

Hopefully, your awareness will be drawn to the **Heartfelt Connections.** These transformative tools will illuminate those who have left a positive mark on your life. They begin with *You are...* statements. You will be asked to identify the person or people who come to mind when you encounter these *You are...* statements. Keep track of who these Connections are and let them know what they mean to you. Be this Connection for yourself and for others.

Heed Your Heart Questions

In reviewing my journals, I discovered that I had posed many questions. Some of these **Questions** have evolving answers and some require a continuing search. Since these questions have been of value to me, I have included them for you to ponder. These mindful **Questions** are designed to stimulate introspection and/or discussion. When you come upon the list of **Heed Your Heart Questions**, pay attention to the patterns that emerge as you answer them. These inner responses are often the most valuable.

Blissful Heart Activities

One of the key lessons I have learned about myself is that I need time to recharge, to reflect, and to integrate what I have encountered and learned. The **Blissful Heart Activities** provide some of the quickest means I have found to rejuvenate and re-energize. My hope is that as you explore the activities, they will inspire you to devise your own refreshing techniques.

At first you may be perplexed at the **Blissful Heart** portion of each chapter. Please be willing to give the imaginative activities a try, with the understanding that they are created to relax you, to ground you, to recharge your brain and to stir your imagination.

Heart Qualities

You will note that each chapter identifies for you a list of selected **Heart Qualities** that share some commonality. These too are *Intangible Gifts*, in the form of traits you may possess or admire. Use these qualities to get you started on your own path to creating **Heart Messages**.

Heart Messages

Your alertness should intensify as you come to the segment within each chapter that provides scripted examples of *Heart Messages*. Examine these *Heart Messages*, which are designed to assist you in identifying the qualities you value in the people you encounter in your everyday life, including those relationships that are closest to you. They will serve as examples of how to express your feelings and insights more effectively, and they will generate momentum for the next step in the process.

Although I wrote these *Heart Messages* while envisioning particular people who have enriched my life, please read them as if they were intended just for you, the Reader.

Engage Your Heart

These self enhancement exercises are the place for you to personalize and create your own *Heart Messages* by following the suggestions in *Engage your Heart*.

We all know what it means to be engaged. Or do we?

To be engaged in every action and decision we make is not a behavior that we are often taught to exhibit. The purpose of this section is to remind you to *Engage your Heart* each time you create a *Heart Message*. Each chapter will provide different techniques that will enable you to become more adept in the practice of creating *Heart Messages*. In order to complete this section, utilize the *Heartfelt Qualities* that are provided for you.

Encouragements From the Heart

These are intended as a summary of the key concepts provided within each chapter. They will highlight the major points and will allow you to quickly reference and review key concepts.

My philosophy of life, which is to "Bring out the best in others," reverberates throughout the length of this book. I hope that as you turn the pages, your own philosophies will become more apparent.

By all means, add your notations regarding the ideas that resonate with you.

If you permit these *Encouragements From the Heart* to capture your attention, you will find that they will propel you forward.

Now that you are aware of how to proceed within each chapter, Just turn the page.

Open Your Heart

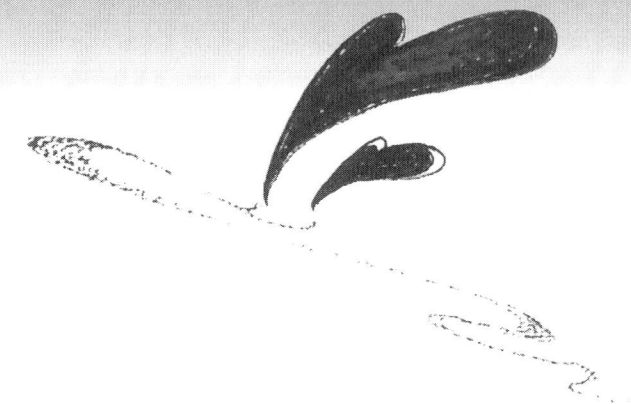

Heart Intentions

Be open to loving deeply, feeling deeply.

Be open to a new way of seeing.

An *Open Heart* builds Connections by being approachable and inclusive.
Its focal point is making others feel welcomed.
It may break, but it will mend.
Its message will be full of wonder and discovery.
When it presents itself, we feel embraced.

Be Open to:

New Approaches

New Experiences

New Perspectives

New Ideas

New Possibilities

New Ways of Thinking and Doing

Fulfilling Your Heart's Desires

Within the past year, name one new approach, one new experience, one new perspective, one new idea or one new possibility that you have at least considered.

Say "Hello" With Your Eyes

Heart Companion: *Bring Along your Smile.*

Heart Tales

Were you ever shy? When I was 12, I certainly was. I had just moved to a new school in a new town, half way through the year. I didn't know how to begin to make new friends. It was then that I heard a piece of advice that I have never forgotten, *Be the one to smile first.* So I began imagining smiles. Then I tried smiling first. The responses I received were immediate and rewarding. People smiled back. What a revelation. I suddenly became approachable. This all happened without my having to say a word. I wondered, what if I was the first to greet others? Could I expect an even warmer reception? I came to realize that the answer is, **Of course**.

Now I hear young mothers utilizing a parenting technique by encouraging their children to **Say "Hello" With Their Eyes** when they are introduced.

This is a very effective non-verbal way to communicate: I am present. I am curious and intrigued by what may happen next. I am interested in who you are and who you could become in my life.

This is my Intangible Gift to you, my Greeting.

Bring Along your smile, **Say "Hello" With Your Eyes** and let me introduce you to a concept that has the potential to transform your interactions into spirit lifting and gratifying experiences, as well as to elevate the tone of your conversations: *The Greeting*.

It is amazingly simple to include *The Greeting* as a daily practice. All you have to do is remember how to begin, over and over again. Please give it a try and notice the incredible difference it makes in your relationships.

We often refer to *The Greeting* as simply a social nicety or necessity. It is, in fact, one of the major factors in determining the degree of success and pleasure we derive from any interaction.

Long ago I heard that the first four minutes of any encounter sets the mood and the tone for the remainder of that exchange. In my experience, this holds true.

The way we greet each other becomes critically important. An automatic exchange of **Hi's, Hello's and What's New**, rarely is sufficient. What is required is a conscious welcoming. The manner in which a conversation begins will determine how it will end.

Open Your Heart - Heart Tales

Certainly a reprimand of, **Why haven't you called?** or **It's about time you got here**, will not result in a harmonious conversation. How much better would we feel if the *Greeting* were, **I'm so glad you called. I've been wanting to talk to you.** Or, **I was getting anxious that you were so late. Is everything OK?**

Can't you just think of a million of these remarks that really push your buttons?

In my observations, the manner in which we *Greet* one another matters, regardless of whether you are meeting someone for the first time, keeping a business appointment, mingling with social acquaintances, talking with your best friend, waking up next to your spouse of many years or communicating with your children. The first four minutes will determine the type and the tone of the experience you will share.

So pause for a moment and *Open Your Heart* to these ideas before you engage with someone and you will be better able to fulfill your Heart's desires.

Think how you want to begin this portion of your relationship.

Be conscious of your **Heart Intention**. Is it to be welcoming?

Be aware of the kind of interaction you want to create. It could be conversational, informative, inquisitive, or even confrontational. Remember that you are able to determine the tone you will set and the impact you will have by the manner in which you approach the first four minutes.

We all want to be welcomed, to be given our own special *Greeting*. When we announce, **I'm here**, we clearly want someone, in addition to the pet, to drop everything and come running.

Offering a *Greeting* will make it easier to cope with whatever comes next.

Remember to *Greet* yourself as well.

What are your first words to yourself upon awakening in the morning?

Are they words of kindness?

Are they gentle?

Are they filled with appreciation and encouragement?

If Opening Your Heart by Greeting the day and yourself with pleasure can influence how the remaining hours will unfold, then why not Open Your Heart before you open your eyes?

Open Your Heart - Heart Tales

Heartfelt Connections

Are you ready for the Heartfelt Connections segment of this chapter?

You will recognize it by the phrase *You are…*

Yes, *You Are So You!* but now is the time to shift your focus to a particular person in your life and hold that person in your Heart as you identify your Connections.

When you come upon the *You are…* phrases, it is your opportunity to elaborate on the part she/he has played in supporting you. Name the person that is best described by each *You are…* phrase. It may be an individual or a group from your past, as well as your present: a parent, a child, a significant other, a relative, a teacher, a work colleague, or your best friend.

If you find that no one comes to mind, it probably means that you would benefit from finding someone like this to invite into your life.

Be sure to include your own name in the list of potential considerations. Maybe you are the one who performs this role for others and for yourself. If you become the *You are…*, you may discover that the rest of your world will respond in kind.

Each of the continuing chapters will also include a portion entitled: **Heartfelt Connections** where you will be asked to complete the phrase: *You are…* by identifying who this person is in your life.

You are the Gentle Eyes that Welcome Me.

You accept and include me,
You make me feel significant and valued.
You welcome the essence of who I am.

Who is this person in your life?

Heed Your Heart Questions

Use these mindful questions to kindle introspection and discussion.

If you desire to add to the happiness of another, then change their Heart with a Smile and reveal their Intangible Gifts.

Someone you know has just appeared.
Set your imaginary stage.

Be the *Gentle Eyes* that welcomes them.
How will your *Open Heart* approach the first four minutes of this encounter?
How do you want to begin?
Are you able to focus your full attention?
Are you smiling?
Are you saying, *"Hello" with your eyes*?
How do you make others feel welcomed?
What steps do you take to appear approachable?

What is your Greeting?

What advice has made a difference in your life?
In what ways have you tried to follow this advice?
How has this advice enriched your experiences?

Blissful Heart Activities

Please don't skip the **Blissful Heart Activities**.

They are represented in each chapter and are designed to engage you, relax you, and rejuvenate you.

Sometimes they are silly.

Try being the one to Smile First for a day.

Observe how many **smile back** responses you receive.

Smile first as you look at yourself in the mirror.

Smile first at your family.

Smile first at your friends.

Smile first at work

Make a smile your initial *Greeting* in the first four minutes.

Pause.

See what happens.

Welcoming Heart Qualities

These Qualities are *Intangible Gifts* that relate to the topic in this chapter. Feel free to use these descriptors to help you write your own **Heart Messages**.

Naturally you can change them into other forms of speech.

For Example: Invites, inviting, invitation, invitingly

Invites
Includes
Initiates
Greets
Welcomes
Makes space
Finds time
Accepts
Treasures
Gentle
Charming

Open
Kind
Gracious
Warm
Generous
Entertaining
Giving
Social
Approachable
Networks

Heart Messages

Wouldn't it be wonderful to uplift your life and the lives of others?

One of the simplest ways to transform your relationships is to spotlight for people the best versions of themselves. I'm sure that you are familiar with the concept of praise. There is the Hallelujah of Praise on one end of the continuum, but there is the equally important simple acknowledgment of someone's presence on the other end. Compliments of course, would qualify as praise. Admiration, recognition, acknowledgment, reassurance, validation, giving credit, providing feedback, appreciation, applause and constructive criticism all fit inside the parameters of praise.

Yes, anytime you say something well intentioned and uplifting, it is a form of praise. Indeed, you are giving an *Intangible Gift*. This *Intangible Gift* can become a **Heart Message**.

Creating a **Heart Message** is a way to express the qualities you admire in others, to share the positive impact they have imparted, and to define how their *Intangible Gifts* have made your life more meaningful.

If you sometimes keep the special notes of gratitude that people have sent you, if you occasionally re-read the affirming paragraphs in recommendations that people have written about you, if you consciously choose to associate with those friends who make you feel worthwhile, if you comment on the positive traits you observe in family and friends, then you are familiar with **Heart Messages**.

A **Heart Message** is a way to share with others how you feel about them and what they mean to you.

Hearing genuine words from the Heart makes us all feel lighter, more confident, more aligned and more nourished.

All those uplifting vibrations can result in a rush of well being, an expansive smile, or an impulse to do something amazing.

Anticipate how much delight you will derive from recreating those feeling in others.

Imagine watching a smile emerge on someone's face as your unique form of Intangible Gift, a Heart Message, is received.

Open Your Heart - Heart Messages

Read the following **Heart Messages** to get ideas. The samples utilize the list of **Heartfelt Qualities**.

They are designed to assist you in creating your own **Heart Messages**. Within this section, they all relate to: *You are the Gentle Eyes that Welcome Me*.

When I think of those people in my life whose *Gentle Eyes* welcome me, the following **Heart Messages** come to mind. As you read them imagine that they are meant for you. Let them boost your spirits.

Receive these *Intangible Gifts* with an *Open Heart*.

✔**Check the ones that best describe you.**

★**Put a star next to the ones that describe the person or people that you have identified as** *the Gentle Eyes that Welcome You*.

Put initials next to the star if you have more than one person that welcomes you.

You have a talent for making me feel included in any conversation.

I recognize that you are usually the one who initiates our getting together.

How is it that you always have time for me? It makes me feel so welcome.

Your skill at entertaining is reflected in the warm, enchanting settings you create.

I am constantly impressed by the way you make everyone, especially me, feel as if they are the most treasured person in your life.

I'm so glad you called. I have been saving up things to share with you.

You are so good at single mingling, meeting new people and finding a common ground. You put everyone at ease.

You seem to fit in to any group.

Your gracious manner makes you so approachable and draws us all to you.

You turn a favor to me into a gift for you.

Open Your Heart - Heart Messages

Engage Your Heart

You may recall hearing that positive energy has the power to revitalize us. The more positive energy we absorb, the more confident we are.

Sending Heart Messages is a means of conveying your positive thoughts into positive energy. It is about empowering others, not holding power over them.

Share a **Heart Message**,

Not because you are trying to manipulate or modify the behavior of others, not because you wish to use flattery to advance yourself, and not because you are fishing for compliments, but purely because you want to give a gift that only you can give, an *Intangible Gift* from your Heart, a **Heart Message**.

If the idea of helping people to unfold and reveal their strengths and talents appeals to you, then participating in the **Engage your Heart** segment of each chapter will be your opportunity to play a role in shaping their lives.

Looking for the positive in others will become a habit that will allow you to focus on both the external accomplishments you observe and the internal satisfactions you feel.

Feel free to toy with various ideas. Some may be down to earth, some quixotic. This is a place to experiment, a place for new ways of thinking and doing. Put aside your inner critic and *Open Your Heart* to whatever pops into your mind. There is no need to aspire to perfection, so just let your imagination soar.

What you put your attention on grows!

Create Heart Messages which include constructive thoughts that will leave others with a sense of balance and clarity.

Open Your Heart - Engage Your Heart

You are the Gentle Eyes that Welcome Me.

Each of us recognizes this look in our own way. For me, it was the look in my mother's eyes.
I have found that same look in the eyes of friends and other caring people.
It always makes me feel cherished.

One time I discovered that look **and** those same green eyes on the face of a man that I didn't recognize. He was, in fact, my mother's brother, my uncle, whom I hadn't seen for over 25 years. His appearance had changed, but not his eyes. To my surprise, I heard these words come out of my mouth, "You are looking at me like I should hug you."

Who says this to a perceived stranger?
I did.
It was because I knew those eyes.
They were the same ones that had welcomed me my entire life, my mother's eyes.

So be on the look out for the *Gentle Eyes that Welcome You.*
They come in various colors and shapes, but they have in common that *Welcoming Look.*

What **Heart Companions**, *in addition to a smile, do you Bring Along when you Greet those Gentle Eyes?*

Open Your Heart - Engage Your Heart

Now it is your turn to **Engage Your Heart** by weaving your **Heart Messages** into the daily patterns of your experience.

Think of those people in your life who are the *Gentle Eyes that Welcome You*. Begin with them.

Use the **Welcoming Heart Qualities** to help you identify the *Intangible Gifts* that you would like to share with those people who are your *Gentle Eyes*.

Write the name of each person here:

Share your **Heart Messages** here:

Open Your Heart - Engage Your Heart

Encouragements From the Heart

Each **Encouragement** segment begins with a reference to a Heart in the **Heart Intentions**, is followed by an *Intangible Gift* and continues with reminders to include your *Bring Along* companion, as well as your **Heart Connection**, to your encounters. Varying approaches for bringing out the best in others are summarized and pertinent sayings and quotes are provided as memory tools.

Heart Intentions
Open Your Heart to loving deeply, feeling deeply.
Be Open to a new way of seeing.

Intangible Gift
Your *Greeting*.

Bring Along
Your *Smile* as your companion.

Heart Connection
Be the *Gentle Eyes* that Welcome.

Take Aways
Greet yourself.
Be the first to smile.
Say "Hello" With Your Eyes.
Incorporate **Welcoming Qualities** into your *Greeting*.
Use the first four minutes to set the tone of each encounter.
The way you begin a conversation is the key to how it will end.
Transform your positive thoughts into positive energy.
As you nourish certain qualities in your own life, they will flourish in your relationships too.
Create a habit of including **Heart Messages** in your daily conversation.
What you put your attention on grows.
Identify what advice has influenced you.

"You never get a second chance to make a first impression."
Peter Galbraith

Reveal Your Heart

Heart Intentions

Reveal your Heart to those you cherish and trust.

Unveil your hopes and dreams.

A *Revealed Heart* deepens Connections by sharing its passions and emotions.
It spotlights compatible beliefs, values, and aspirations.
It will be vulnerable, but it can create a lasting bond.
It will send a message of trust and confidence.
When it offers itself, we feel cherished.

Have you ever had difficulty Revealing Your Heart?

Imagine designing a **Revealed Heart** that mirrors the feelings and emotions that your Heart contains.

What would your Revealed Heart look like?

Would your Heart open like a book or be locked and require a key?

Would it require assembly and include directions?

Would it emerge layer by layer until the core essence was exposed?

Would it expand like an accordion or contain many compartments?

Would it expose your innermost fears?

How would you describe your Revealed Heart to someone you love?

When you *Reveal Your Heart*,
it gives others the opportunity to take a similar risk by revealing her/his Heart,
which may result in deepening your relationship.
It is a chance you take with people you cherish and trust.

Remember to *Prepare Your Heart* to accept whatever the response may be.

Fond

Heart Companion: *Bring Along your Confidence.*

Heart Tales

He: Considerate and reserved on the Outside,
A Kid at Heart on the Inside.

She: Outgoing and independent on the Outside,
Tenderhearted on the Inside.

She: "We have been dating for a long time and I really need to know where our relationship is going and where I stand."

He: "But my Dear, you know that I am very fond of you."

She: **FOND!** Fond is what you are of your dog.

He: "Oh no, I **LOVE** my dog!

The moment when we know in our Hearts exactly how we feel about a relationship and the level of commitment we are willing to extend does not always make a spontaneous appearance. There are times when we are reluctant to express our emotions, so we hide our true feelings for fear they will be ridiculed or unreciprocated.

He and **She** have been married now for many years, because **She** was an irresistible force, ablaze with the *Intangible Gift* of *Enthusiasm*. By being the first to reveal her hopes and dreams, **She** instilled a confidence in their future together.

She *Revealed Her Heart.*

She became the **"Yes"** in his hesitation.

Heartfelt Connections

You are the "Yes" in my hesitation.

You make me believe that I CAN do it.
You help me to feel confident, self-assured, empowered, and ready to commit.
You encourage me to step forward.

Who alleviates your fears?
Write his/her name here.

Heed Your Heart Questions

What causes us to hesitate?
Often it is a component of the **FUD** factor: Fear, Uncertainty, and Doubt.

There are occasions, especially if our past choices have not served us well, when a feeling of hesitation engulfs us; because above all we do not want to make a mistake. It is at these times we seek the assurance that we can choose wisely. It is helpful when someone shows us an alternative to jumping in feet first or taking tentative baby steps. Assessing how supported we feel in those moments of hesitation is reflected in our response. It is then that we look to the person who is the **"Yes"** in our hesitation. Is it the face you see in the mirror?

Next time you feel hesitant, it may be helpful to ask yourself:

What do I fear?

What am I uncertain about?

What is causing my uncertainty?

What are my doubts?

What could someone do to encourage me?

With whom do I share my hopes and dreams?

*What motivates us to reply "Yes"
to a new phase of our life or an untried experience?*

How could you respond differently the next time you feel hesitant?

Can you be FUD free for 20 seconds?

Say **"YES".**

**What if your *Revealed Heart* Intention
was to examine your hesitations and to unveil your hopes?**

What do your answers reveal about your Heart?

Can you locate the space in your Heart that answers "Yes"?

Blissful Heart Activity

Raise your hand and yell, "Pick me, Pick me!"

Reveal what is in your Heart by creating a Heart Space for a feeling you are fond of.

What have you imagined?
Think of a feeling you want to invite into your Heart Space.
My most recent invitation was for a feeling of Joie de Vie (Joyfulness).

What feeling did you invite into your Heart Space?
Shake your head **Yes** 3 times.

What feeling are you hesitant to invite in?
Shake your head **No** 3 times.
Shake your head **Yes** 3 more times.
Which Shake, Yes or No, felt bolder, better, fonder?

Tell a **Heart Tale** *about a time you said* **"Yes"** *to one of your hesitations.*

Say "Yes to Life" Heart Qualities

Here are some qualities that focus on getting you to reply **"Yes"** to life's experiences!

Motivating

Stimulating

Inspiring

Spontaneous

Encouraging

Enthusiastic

Exuberant

Self Assured

Confident

Committed

Empowered

Curious

Heart Messages

Just to get you started, I have finished these *You Are the "Yes" in my Hesitation* messages by selecting one of the **Say "Yes to Life" Qualities**.

For example:

1. When you reveal your hopes and dreams, it makes me realize how much we have in common.

2. Your enthusiasm is infectious.
   It uplifts my heart and makes me feel like I am capable of anything.

3. Your self assurance seems obvious, because you are always up for trying something new.

4. You know just what to do to motivate me.

5. The way you join unrelated ideas inspires me to be more creative.

6. You bring out the best in me.

7. Your confidence in me empowers me to stretch beyond my comfort zone.

8. A young child has that same sense of wonder and lack of inhibition that you do.
   Your exuberance encourages me to be more playful.

9. Often when we speak, I find myself energized to tackle something challenging.

10. You never hesitate to do the unplanned or unexpected. When I resist, you are there with a big dose of spontaneity to propel me along a more exciting path.

11. You remind me to say "Yes" to my dreams.

12. You challenge me to reach a bit further each day.
    You are living proof that no matter how many times we reinvent ourselves, each time we have an opportunity to grow.

13. Your example has taught me that it is never too late to pursue a new passion.

Engage Your Heart

Using the previous cues and examples, create a Heart Message for the person who is the "Yes" in your hesitation, by completing the following sentences yourself.

For example: After we have been together I feel… (Complete the sentence)

1. You know just what to do to…

2. You inspire me to…

3. I admire the way…

4. You bring out…

5. You have a way of…

6. Your enthusiasm is…

7. You encourage me to…

8. I find myself inspired and energized to…

9. When I resist you are there with a big dose of…

10. You remind me to say "YES" to …

11. You challenge me…

Encouragements From the Heart

Heart Intentions
Reveal Your Heart to those you cherish and trust.
Unveil your hopes and dreams.

Intangible Gift
Your *Enthusiasm*.

Bring Along
Your *Confidence*.

Heart Connection
Be the "**Yes**".

Take Aways

Enthusiasm and Encouragement sway more Hearts.

Practice being **FUD** free.

Create space in your Heart.

Invite in what your Heart desires.

Take the initiative.

Add to the *"Yes to Life"* **Qualities** list.

Change one thing. That is imagination.

Rehearse your dreams, not your fears.

Timing is the key to good communication.

Commit to one of your hesitations.

Reveal Your Heart!

"Only when one is connected to one's inner core is one connected to others."
Anne Morrow Lindbergh

Believing Heart

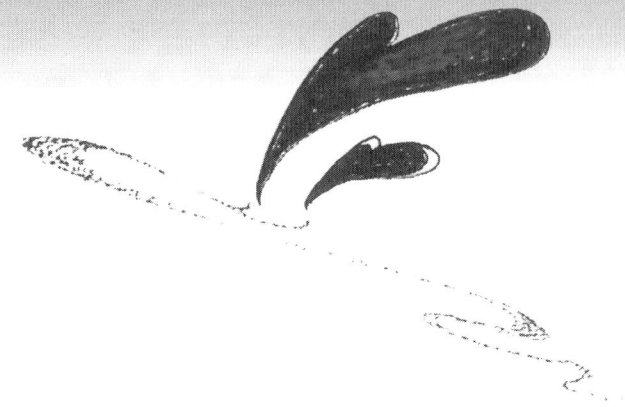

Heart Intentions

A Believing Heart highlights for others the best versions of themselves.

Applaud the efforts of those you believe in.

A *Believing Heart* strengthens Connections by bringing out the best in others.
Its focus is on inner beauty and character.
It will not waiver.
Its message will be authentic and insightful.
When it shows itself, we feel supported.

Mirror, Mirror on the Wall...

When we ask, *"Who is the fairest of them all?"*
we know what we want the answer to be.

Yet there are occasions when we tell ourselves that we could not possibly
be the fairest, most desirable, most lovable, smartest, cleverest, bravest:
Well, you get the point.

It is times like these that we may not want to hear, *You Are So You!*

What we really need when our self-esteem needs boosting
is a *Believing Heart* to act as our *Reflecting Mirror*.

We need someone who can see the image of ourselves
that we have obscured by self-doubt.

What we want is someone who knows our flaws,
but accepts us for who we are, someone whose belief in us is unshaken,
someone who validates our strengths.

We need a *Reflecting Mirror* who helps us arrive at a more
positive perception of ourselves, a perception which allows us
to look in the Mirror and view the true reflection of who we are.

Having people who believe in us nurtures a sense of belonging.
Identifying those relationships that cheer us on and seeking
their support can make a remarkable difference in
how we approach the challenges we set for ourselves.

Turning Green (Not an Environmental Statement)

Heart Companion: Bring Along Limitless Possibilities.

Heart Tales

Swirling, swishing, spiraling sensations enveloped me.

I was being suspended by a water treatment specialist in an outdoor pool under the red rocks of Sedona, but I was unable to tell if my body was floating in the sky blue water or soaring in the blue sky overhead.

It was a profound experience, but when the relaxation session ended, I found that I was suddenly very dizzy and suffering from motion sickness. I had to be helped back to the spa lounge, where I lay down on the sofa and inwardly pleaded for the room to stop spinning.

The next thing I remember was my friend appearing by my side and commenting on what a lovely shade of green I was. Relieved to see her, I assumed that she had come to stay with me until I felt better.

Much to my surprise, she handed me my things and insisted that we were not going to miss out on the private tour we had booked. When I protested, she said, "Oh, I have seen you go on in much worse shape than this. You'll be just fine in a bit."

She was right.

By the time we arrived at our destination, my disorientation had disappeared. If she hadn't been there to remind me of how persevering I could be, I would have missed a fabulous experience. The fact that she had seen me soldier on in worse conditions and therefore knew I could manage this situation, was the strength I needed.

Sometimes we just need a helping hand and sometimes we need a little shove and sometimes we need a kick in the pants. Those who truly know us, know how far to push. They are the ones who see the strength in us unspent.

They are our Reflecting Mirrors.

They reflect back to us our Intangible Gifts, our Inner Beauty and Strength.

Heartfelt Connections

You are my Reflecting Mirror.

You reflect back to me my brightest radiance.
You see my Inner Beauty.
You recognize the strength in me unspent.
You know the treasured parts of me that others may not see.

Who believes in who you are and all you can become?

Heed Your Heart Questions

When you look in the mirror do you see your own *Inner Beauty*?

What image are you trying to project?

What makes you feel attractive, desirable, confident and vibrant?

What do you do that promotes these feelings about yourself?

Do you believe that Beauty on the inside shines through?

What qualities do you admire about yourself that you hope others will observe as well?

What do you want your *Reflecting Mirror* to see?

Do you act as a *Reflecting Mirror* for others?

When your *Believing Heart* **Intention** focuses on the inner beauty and strength in others, rather than results and accomplishments, it becomes easier to applaud people's efforts.

Do you make it a habit to look for the *Inner Beauty* in others?

Consider this Limitless Possibility:

What if you decided to quit being an oyster and decided to become a pearl?

Whose *Believing Heart* would support your decision?

Blissful Heart Activity

Oh Baby, Baby!

A dear Aunt, who was visiting us on her 80th Birthday, appeared in a beautiful multicolored silk dress for a special evening out. She looked so attractive that I decided an amateur photo shoot was in order. At first, she posed very properly and primly. Although the shots were lovely, they just didn't seem to capture her personality.

"Let's continue outside," I suggested.
" Try walking up and down the deck, and pretend it is a stage."

As she began to move, I coaxed her along by saying,

Oh baby, baby.

You look fantastic!

Wow, that smile is beautiful.

Do that again.

Toss your hair.

Give me a flirty look.

And right there in front of my camera eyes, she was transformed into the vivacious young woman I'm sure that she had been at 20 something. She became the woman who had joined the Red Cross and had received a medal for her brave actions while driving an ambulance during World War II. For those brief photo moments, she was not elderly and grey, but vibrant and glowing like the colors of her silk. Her *Inner Beauty* had eclipsed all remnants of age.

Describe how someone has reflected your Inner Beauty back to you.

In order to persuade your *Inner Beauty* to surface, find a way to coax the **You** of younger days out to play. It is often in those playful times that the essence of who we really are shines through.

Believing Heart Qualities

Inner beauty

Character

Integrity

Authentic

Wise

Strength   *Attractive*

Insightful   *Elegant*

Vibrant   *Desirable*

Glowing   *Approachable*

Radiant   *Youthful*

Distinctive   *Witty*

                           Clever

                           Funny

                           Sweet

                           Bright

Heart Messages

Which would you rather hear from your Reflecting Mirror?

Feedback: I like your outfit.

Reassurance: The cut of that jacket is very flattering on you.

Acknowledgment: Is that a new outfit?

Compliment: Your wardrobe selections reflect your good taste.

Validation: I think it is your unique combination of colors and the way in which you accessorize every outfit that makes your appearance seem so polished.

Admiration: People seek you out because they admire your fashion sense.

Recognition: You have definitely developed your own style.

Appreciation: I so appreciate that you dressed up for this special occasion.

Heart Message: Your flair for combining patterns, colors and textures has inspired me to experiment with my own wardrobe.

The difference between our usual definition of praise and a Heart Message lies in being specific regarding the Intangible Gifts the person possesses, and the ways in which these Gifts have influenced, inspired or impacted you.

People love details about themselves, so cite specific examples of their appealing traits, as you have observed them in action.

Being more specific is the way that you can personalize your **Heart Messages** and make them genuinely from your Heart.

These are the kinds of Intangible Gifts that attract our attention.

Believing Heart - Heart Messages

What would you like to hear from your Reflecting Mirrors?

When you project your strengths, they gain momentum and become more powerful. Your image of yourself influences how others see you. Identify your best qualities and share them.

If you find it difficult to tell others what you like most about yourself, try experimenting with Imaginary *Reflecting Mirrors* and let them speak on your behalf. You may be surprised at what they will divulge.

Here are some examples of **Heart Messages** that I would like *Imaginary Reflecting Mirrors* to say:

Wishful Examples:
I know I can count on you, because you have a quick mind, a trusting nature and a cool head in an emergency. You are persevering, dependable and organized. You know how to get things done under pressure and you are tougher and stronger than you look.

You are eager for new adventures, ready to explore some unknown place or topic. You are so adept at combining the two aspects of your character: One, the responsible, practical you, who is capable of exhibiting classic composure and Two, the you that loves to flirt with danger and excitement. I can tell that you would be willing to travel on a moment's notice to exotic lands. No wonder you are so good at making things up as you go along.

You seem to have a very sensitive, caring side that shows through whenever nature surrounds you. You have a great eye for detail and a delightful sense of wonder, coupled with a desire to impart your knowledge and enthusiasm. You love learning new facts and ideas and sharing them with others.

How quickly you get to the core of a matter. When you interact with people, you aren't distracted by outward impressions, so you can see the essence of who they really are. You seem to have a sixth sense of what to ask and when to ask it. You time your observations to occur when others are receptive and you have the ability to size up a situation accurately and instantaneously. I value your insights.

What would you like your Believing Hearts to say to you?

Believing Heart - Heart Messages

Engage Your Heart

Imagine what your Reflecting Mirrors would want to hear.

Use the **Believing Heart Qualities** to create your own **Heart Messages**:

Reflecting Mirror Cues:

1. Express how their actions or behaviors make you feel.
2. Compliment the inner qualities they possess that you admire.
3. Describe one of these qualities in even more detail. Remember to be specific.
4. Feel free to combine any of the following statements into an even more specific **Heart Message**.

Fill in the missing specifics in these samples to create your own **Heart Messages** for your *Reflecting Mirror*:

Your contribution (which is?) means so much because . . .

You make such a difference by . . .

You enrich my life in the following ways . . .

You make me happy when you . . .

I feel safe when you . . .

My heart goes thump, thump, thump when . . .

From the moment I met you, I . . .

You are so receptive to new approaches, solutions and ideas.
I especially recall the time you . . .

He is a true entrepreneur, just like you.
You both have that same wonderful sense of vision and . . .

I am sure you still look . . . , as I always picture you in my Heart.

page 47

Encouragements From the Heart

Heart Intention
A *Believing Heart* highlights for others the best versions of themselves.
Applaud the efforts of those you believe in.

Intangible Gift
Your *Inner Beauty*.

Bring Along
The traits that you want your *Believing Heart* to possess. There are *Limitless Possibilities*.

Heart Connection
Be the *Reflecting Mirror* that reflects back the best in others.

Take Aways
Itemize the contents of your *Believing Heart*. Are there any beliefs that no longer serve you well?

Believe in yourself.

Suspend your disbelief.

Let your own *Inner Beauty* shine through.

Base your decisions on the qualities that you value.

Personalize your **Heart Messages** by being more specific.

Create Fantasy *Reflecting Mirrors*, if no real life ones are available when you need them.

Pretend. It is a way of remembering who we are.

As you nourish certain qualities in your own life, they will flourish in your relationships too.

View life through a lens of appreciation.

Strengthen your Connections by focusing on the *Inner Beauty* you recognize in others.

"Being deeply loved by someone gives you strength. Loving someone deeply gives you courage."
Lao Tzu

Ways to personalize your **Heart Messages**

Begin with Gratitude.

Be clear about your intentions.

Express specific qualities you admire or value.

Showcase the inner qualities someone possesses.

Highlight people's *Intangible Gifts*.

Cite examples of times and places
in which you have observed the person exhibiting the qualities you admire.

Identify your emotional response to a particular action
or behavior and describe how it made you feel.

Elaborate on the impact words or deeds have had upon you.

Share the ways in which you have been motivated, inspired or influenced.

Enumerate on how your life has been enriched.

Be genuine.

Articulate your observations.

Adoring Heart

Heart Intentions

Show your Adoring Heart to the people you love.

Extend your respect, recognition, and approval.

An *Adoring Heart* enhances Connections by holding positive expectations.
It sees others through a lens of appreciation.
It will overflow with joy.
Its message will radiate unconditional delight.
When it speaks to us, it is in the language of Love.

Catch someone doing something good.

When you grace others with your *Adoring Heart* Messages,
make sure you are being sincere.

Heart Messages only work if they come from a genuine place of appreciation
and delight, a place of adoring, a place of respect and acceptance,
not from a place of manipulation.

As you get in the habit of noticing the fascinating, entertaining, clever, endearing, ingenious behaviors of those you care about and interact with, you will find that you begin to overlook the little annoyances and idiosyncrasies that come with each of us as human beings.

Regardless of how self-assured others may appear, the manner in which you champion who they are and what they do affects their level of confidence, especially if you are someone who holds their respect.

Make someone a Favorite for a day.

Shower your Favorite with Intangible Gifts.

I'd Do Anything for a *Good Boy*

Heart Companion: *Bring Along your Approval.*

Heart Tales

"What did you name your new puppy?" my niece asked.

"Namche," I replied. "I understand it means mountain in Nepalese."

Her retort was: "My mommy said you would name it something weird."

Perhaps the dog agreed, because he thought his name was *Good Boy*.

We doted on our first puppy. Everything he did was adorable and we were besotted. We never considered obedience school, because he was perfect in our eyes. When he went to the front door and gave us his **I'm ready look**, we said *Good Boy!* When he greeted us, tail wagging and pure pleasure in his expression, we said, We missed you so much, because you are such a *Good Boy!* When he waited patiently to play ball, while we finished whatever we deemed important, we said, *Good Boy!* There were even moments when he was elevated to *Angel Boy!* status.

Are there people in your life who might do anything for a Good Boy?

Is it possible that there are occasions when we aren't looking with our Hearts at the people we love? And if so, why is that?

Is it that being compassionate towards a pet is easier?

Are our standards for those who matter to us so high that we forget about the language of love?

Do we need to cut our loved ones a little slack?

Do we get caught up in the many tasks at hand and ignore the joy around us?

Are we so focused on our own agendas, including getting things done and making things perfect or better, that we don't see the perfection in front of us?

Adoring Heart - Heart Tales

Have you ever fallen into the habit of pointing out the imperfections of others or the things that could be improved upon?

I hope it isn't just me.

Instead, let's try catching one another doing something good.

What would it take for someone to receive a *Good Boy* or *Good Girl* from you?

Bring Along your Approval and grant the people around you a *Good Boy!* or a *Good Girl!* as often as you can.

Your *Positive Expectations* are an *Intangible Gift.*
Anticipate that everything will turn out by clarifying what pleases you and makes you happy.

Would that feel better?

Positive Expectations turn into positive results.

We all recognize Scolding Looks, our own included, but don't you think we'd really rather be wagging our tails?

Adoring Heart - **Heart Tales**

Heartfelt Connections

You are the Scolding Look I Pay Attention to.

You help me to examine my behavior;
You push my buttons, and make me try harder.
You hold Positive Expectations of me and we seek each other's Approval.

Whose opinions really matter to you?

Heed Your Heart Questions

Whose recognition is most important to you?

Who in your life do you yearn to hear say, *Good Boy* or *Good Girl?*

Keep in mind, the most valuable opinion is the one you have of yourself.

Do you dote on anyone or anything?

A person's greatest strength, carried to extreme, is their greatest weakness.

What is your greatest strength?

If you carry your strength to the extreme,

What is your greatest weakness?

How are they related?

If your Adoring Heart could ask a question, what would it be?

When you feel disapproving, try extending your respect and recognition for what does please you, and make that your *Adoring Heart* **Intention**.

Blissful Heart Activity

Ask for a Hug, you probably need one about now. If no one is available, give yourself a Hug.

Respond to a Scolding Look with an Adorable Look that will melt their Scoldy Heart.

Good Job Heart Qualities

Organized

Efficient

Competent

Poised

Productive   *Accomplished*

Reliable   *Committed*

Responsible   *Accountable*

Capable   *Contributing*

Convincing   *Helpful*

                                  Talented

                                  Trustworthy

                                  Appreciative

                                  Persevering

Heart Messages

We all have unique strengths and talents, our Super Powers, that are crystal clear to others, which we may not acknowledge as our Intangible Gifts, because they seem effortless to us.

Examine the following **Heart Messages**. They are examples of thoughts you may want to express to various people who are present in your life. As you identify these potential Super Powers, these unique *Intangible Gifts*, quiet the scolding voices and listen to the *Adoring Hearts* instead.

A loved one
When tough choices have to be made, I love that your response is, "We will make this work out together." Your super power is your confidence. You are so comfortable with contradictions and uncertainties. I know that you will smile at me and then I will believe that eventually, everything will turn out.

A boss or colleague
You possess the kind of super power that recognizes when an opportunity arises. Of course you are prepared for opportunity when it presents itself, so you hear it knocking. You consistently seize the chance to learn and to grow. No wonder you are so accomplished.

A parent
Your wisdom reaches us. You share with us the gift of vision for our full potential and the lesson of patience to bring it into focus. You demonstrate what it means to lead a balanced life. Your magic is the way you use your intuition to make decisions. We trust your insights and experience to help us determine our own choices.

The children in your life
Your youthful energy and exuberance make me feel as if I can tackle any project.

A friend
Friends like you and especially you, inspire me to reach for the improbable. Every day I see ways in which you have contributed to our friendship. Your super power is your zest for life and all it has to offer!

Engage Your Heart

Take this opportunity to express the ways in which you see others shine. Divulge their super powers and identify their own special variety of Intangible Gifts.

Send an *Adoring Heart* **Message** to someone you admire.

Go ahead and propose an *Adoring Heart* **Message** for yourself based on the Super Powers you possess.

Select the qualities for which you would most like to be recognized. Write what you wish the following people would say:

You may choose to select from the list of **Heartfelt Qualities** or to pick the qualities for which would most like to be noticed.

A loved one

Your parents

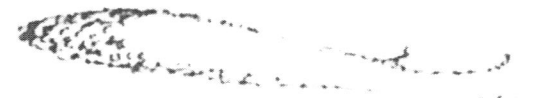

Your boss or colleague

The children in your life

Your friends

Good Job!

Adoring Heart - Engage Your Heart

*Create a Heart Message that highlights
your Favorites' uniqueness.*

What Super Powers or talents do you admire in them?

Tell them about their Intangible Gifts.

Give them an Adoring look.

If **Thank You** doesn't light up their eyes, give them your approval.
Try *Well Done and Good Job!*

Shower them with attention using the **Heartfelt Qualities**
you have practiced and notice the difference in their response to you.

Adoring Heart - **Engage Your Heart**

Encouragements From the Heart

Heart Intentions
Show your *Adoring Heart* to the people you love.
Extend your respect, your recognition and your approval of who they are.

Intangible Gift
Positive Expectations make great *Intangible Gifts*.

Bring Along
Your *Approval*.

Heartfelt Connections
Be Mindful of your *Look* and your *Tone*.

Take Aways
Try on an *Adoring Heart* look when you feel like scolding and watch what transpires.

Positive thoughts create positive feelings. Positive feelings create positive energy.

Expose yourself to positive feelings and energy as frequently as you can.

Find something to dote on.

The most valuable opinion is the one you have of yourself.

Catch someone doing something **good**.

Have a Favorite and shower her or him with a *Good Girl/Boy*.

Spotlight people's greatest strengths. Recognize that it is the positive version of their greatest weakness.

Summon your power.

Be aware of how you choose to define others and yourself.

Take care before speaking.

Our self esteem needs 5 praising experiences to undo one negative comment.

Praise, Affirm, Recognize, Appreciate, Compliment.

"Help others shine, build signal fires, send up flares, throw sparks."
Clarrisa Pincola Estes

Heart Intentions Review

Open Your Heart

An Open Heart is one that is ever expanding into its infinite potential of giving and receiving love. It recognizes its current limitations and takes the necessary steps to remove the blocks, be they grief, guilt or the biggest barrier of all fear, with courage and perseverance. An open heart is yearning to unfold into a greater and greater expression of itself and wanting to discover all that it can be.

The Power of Thank You, Connecting the World Through Gratitude

Dee Dee Boies

Reveal Your Heart

When your Heart is revealed, who is allowed to see it?

Believing Heart

Once I had a poster mounted on my office wall that stated: "Not to Decide, Is to Decide." The phrase was a daily reminder that every action I took required a decision. I could make the decision a conscious choice or leave it to fate, but it did become a decision. It could be a decision that took form in my head, in my gut, or in my Heart, so I had to learn to pay attention to how I generated my decisions. So do you.

Examine your own decision making process and then, just for fun, make a decision based on Beauty.

What did you decide?

Ask your *Believing Heart* how this decision differs from the decisions you normally make.

Adoring Heart

Drum beat for an *Adoring Heart*

Lub Dub, Lub Dub, Lub Dub,
Boom Boom!

Remembering Heart

Heart Intentions

Share the contents of your Remembering Heart with the people who have given meaning to your life.

Be a Reminder.

A *Remembering Heart* maintains Connections by being mindful of the Marks we leave on each other's lives.

It takes a wide-angle view, which reminds us of what is significant and precious from the past.

It will fill in the blanks and provide an alternate version of our story.

Its message will illustrate a different perspective.

When it reminds us, we feel whole.

Heart Memories

Thank goodness friends and family help hold our memories for us.

Their perspectives may differ from our own, but the experiences are still shared.

They remind us of who we were and who we have become.

They see the strengths we possess, the ways in which we have grown, and the impact or influence we may have had on the world.

They hold the collective memories of the day- to- day moments that combine to compile the milestones in our lives.

They hold our Heart Memories for us.

One of our purposes is to be a reminder for each other of what we deem notable and worthwhile in the experiences we have shared.

One of the ways in which we retain our humanity, is by connecting the dots for one another.

Remembering Kind of Gal

Heart Companion: *Bring Along your Heart Memories.*

Heart Tales

Each of our experiences is encoded in memory; the question is how do we access such flashes in time.

A friend was conversing with her four year old grandchild about an upcoming visit to Grandma's house. The little girl had been to visit before, but didn't seem to recollect any of the experiences. In an effort to help her recall, the girl's grandmother repeatedly asked her questions.

Do you remember when:

>We went to the beach?
>
>We played in the snow?
>
>We made cookies?

To each prompt, the grand daughter shook her head, No.

Finally the little girl just couldn't resist replying, "I guess I'm just not a **Remembering Kinda Gal**."

This observation on the part of someone so young seems pretty remarkable to me.

>It made me ask myself,
>Am I a **Remembering Kinda Gal**?

What about you?

Heartfelt Connections

You are my Then and my Now.

You are aware of the Marks you have left on my life.
You recollect the parts of me that make a whole.
You remember moments I can't recall.

Who holds your Heart Memories?

Heed Your Heart Questions

Recollecting the sky

Here is something to ponder: What did the sky look like the day you were born? Describe the color. Were there clouds? What type? Was it clear? Was it stormy? Was it daytime? Were there stars?

I certainly have no idea, and now I have no one left to ask except Google®.

I hope there was a dramatic sunset, and that the sky was brushed with oranges, pinks and purples, but I will have to be content with my imagining, for it just never occurred to me that knowing how the sky looked when I entered the world would some day be significant to me, so I never asked.

What important questions would you like to ask?

What triggers memory for you?
Is it the taste of Madelines, the smell of baking bread, the sight of polka dot socks, the feel of a kiss in the moonlight, or the sound of a hummingbird's wings?

What memories has someone shared with you that make you feel more whole, as if a missing part of you has been retrieved?

Who helps you to feel young again?

Who brings out those exuberant qualities?

Who knows the answer to the questions you never thought to ask?

What cherished moments have you shared with someone?

Remind yourself that the **Intention** of a *Remembering Heart* is to be mindful of the marks it leaves.

What memories are creating Connections that restrict you or are too tight?
Can you loosen your grip?

Blissful Heart Activity

Make a Mark, any mark, right here, right now.

When we allow ourselves to just make marks, it has a way of freeing our analytical brain. Making marks helps us to let go.

Use this activity if you need to feel more grounded. It will transport you to the Here. It may even allow your *Heart Memory* to emerge from the *Then* to reappear in the *Now*.

Your Intangible Gift is the Mark you have left on the lives of others.
Draw a symbol for it.

How has someone left their Mark on your Life?
Draw a different symbol for this Mark.

You leave your Mark by touching someone's life.

Be mindful, because leaving your Mark on someone's Heart is an indelible deed.

Remembering Heart Qualities

Shared experiences

Recollections and memories

Reminder of what you have done and what you've said

Connection to your roots

*Evidence of how you have grown and
how you have stayed the same*

Validation of your experiences

Holds a place for you in time and space

Gives historical perspective

Knew you when

Cherishes

Triggers memories

Heart Messages

These messages are designed to help you access those precious moments in your past that are so worth remembering.

Whenever I hear your voice, I am transported to a time in my life that was so uncomplicated. I surge with energy and the oblivion of self-absorption. Who knew how much fun that could be? I long for the days when we trained for marathons, carried along by our own delightful conversations and the incentive of a frosty beer when we finished.

Often when you speak, it is as if you have an artist's brush and you can create a scene or story in your listener's ear and eye. I either listen in awe for long spaces, or I find myself inspired and want to talk fluidly nonstop in new metaphors or tapped memories.

You are the person who knows some of my secret selves. I am thinking now of the Dancer. This is, in actuality, your identity. It is this memory of you that transforms me into the graceful woman of the 5 Rhythms, where I am once again leaping across your living room pretending to be a ballerina.

How important it is for me that you have known me through so many phases of my life. You recognize the professional me, the entrepreneurial me, the adventuresome me, the explorer me and all the other selves that combine to be the essence of me. Sometimes they seem like a dream, but you help me see their reality.

I just returned from a weekend in the Boundary Waters Canoe Area, where I got to hear the loons again. Some of my most cherished memories are my Loon memories of you. (Pun intended) Do you remember?

I love the reconnection that is happening between us right now.

Although we are apart for spans of time, I often sense the memory of your touch.

I know that I can count on you to continue the decades long ritual of calling me on my Birthday. Time mysteriously reverses during these annual conversations and I am reassured that the 20 something girl of long ago still exists.

You show me that everyday moments in our lives are the precious times; that we need to make each minute count, not just the milestones.

Engage Your Heart

Create Heart Messages intended for the people who share the memories that you treasure.

Think of someone who has known you through many phases of your life. What do you appreciate about the *Then* and the *Now* of your relationship?

Explain why they play such an important role in how you view yourself and your life.

Be a Remembering Kinda Gal or Guy.

Encouragements From the Heart

Heart Intentions
Share the memories of your *Remembering Heart*.
Be a Reminder.

Intangible Gift
Make your *Marks Intangible Gifts* wherever they are found.

Bring Along
Your *Heart Memories* by embracing the **Remembering Heart Qualities**.

Heart Connection
Remember the *Then*. Transform the *Now*.

Take Aways
Leaving your Mark on someone's Heart is often an indelible deed.
Search for the memories that complete you.
Before it is too late, ask questions now of those who hold your Heart Memories.
Give answers to unasked questions you think are important to impart.
Acknowledge precious moments, especially the simple, everyday ones.
Find ways to trigger your memory so that you too can be a **Remembering Kinda Gal or Guy**.
Glimpsing the past may allow you to sneak a peek at the future.
Be conscious of your Connections to the past by remembering how they have influenced you.
Remind others of what is meaningful and valuable from the past.

"It doesn't matter who my father was; it matters who I remember he was."
Anne Sexton

Connect Your Heart

Heart Intentions

Create Connections that enrich the world.

Be aware of who you invite into your Heart.

A *Connecting Heart* consciously selects Connections
that support who and what we wish to invite into our lives.

It clarifies our view of those values and qualities that we hold dear.

It will reach out across time and space.

Its message will link our past, present and our future.

When it surfaces, we feel enriched.

True Connections between people can seem rare, but they are worth searching and striving for because:

We stay well by connecting to each other.

We are ultimately all connected to one another, a fact which is increasingly more obvious in this time of global awareness.

How can we tell if we are truly connecting?

Shall we finish each other's sentences?

Might we predict what the other will select off the menu?

Do we trust one another to make a decision,
because we know to the core what each of us would prefer?

If we were lost, could we find each other?

Do we hold each other's Hearts?

Can we read each other's thoughts?

Can we imagine each other's smiles?

Is it your Heart Intention to enrich your Connections by wishing the best for others?

Calling in Cold

Heart Companion: *Bring Along your Companionship.*

Heart Tales

I no longer have the need to **Call in Cold,** but I still think about it sometimes.

When the temperature continued to register well below zero for 30 days in a row, one of the people I worked with joked about doing just that, **Calling in Cold**. Though the idea certainly appealed to everyone in our department, we never actually did **Call in Cold,** but just thinking of placing such a call gave us a little thrill and made it easier to bundle up and brave the elements.

I miss that camaraderie, the kind that exists when you engage with people who understand that when it gets too cold for too long, you need to have the option of collectively calling in. We haven't seen one another in years, but whenever the thermometer plummets, I can feel their warmth and an inexplicable closeness, despite the elusiveness of time and space.

It has just occurred to me that I have never shared this anecdote with those people from my past.

I hope they don't think that their humor and dedication were inconsequential in my life.

It is past time to reassure them.

Think of people from your past that you have neglected to tell how much they meant to you.

Heartfelt Connections

You are the Thread that Connects our Hearts.

You are the person from my past with whom I want to reconnect.
When the phone rings, I will always answer your call.
We share a surprising sense of entanglement as we journey forward.

Who is this Thread in your life?

Heed Your Heart Questions

In this age of Social Networking, it is important to ask ourselves what kind of Heart Connections we wish to attract.

What kind of Connections do you want to include that are currently missing from your life?

What values and beliefs do you choose to share that will enrich your mutual existence?

Notice what you have in common with the people in your life.

Is it a shared interest?

Is it an approach to life?

Is it a work style that improves the results you wish to achieve?

Is it a similarity in rhythms and pace?

Is it an energy exchange that enhances the time you share and leaves you feeling rejuvenated?

Is it a common belief system or a common Worldview?

Can you count on a certain synchronistic experience occurring and something akin to magic happening when you are together?

Name the Connections.

Blissful Heart Activity

Interlock the fingers of your hands.

Flip your hands over so that you are looking at your fingers.

Now stretch your arms out in front of you.

Feel the Connection to other parts of your body.

Lean Forward.

What is the smallest thing you see?

What is the largest thing you see?

What is the thread that Connects the two?

The smallest thing I saw was a black rock collected from the beach and the largest thing I saw was the sugar pine tree outside my window. The Connection for me is that they are both objects that ground me, because they are linked to the earth and to nature.

And what Connections did you observe?

Connecting Heart Qualities

In Sync
Keeps in touch
Shares philosophy
Common interests
Shared values
Serendipity
There for me
Telepathic
Mood booster
Same wavelength
Gets me
Trusts

Add your **Connecting Heart Qualities:**

Heart Messages

What kind of Connections do you want to include in your life?

Here are some of my *Heart Message* Desires:

I want to include people in my life who enjoy the same delights as I do.

Wouldn't it be great if:

They appreciated the same kind of humor?

They made me laugh and if they thought I was witty and amusing?

Our inner and outer rhythms complemented one another?

Our conversations were so stimulating that we couldn't wait to meet up?

How wonderful it would be if we felt totally comfortable and at ease in each other's company.

Let it be someone who sees with similar eyes the beauty in what exists and who introduces me to new experiences that inspire creativity.

Oh, and please let the mere fact that these people exist somewhere in my Universe, elevate my mood and bring me joy.

I'm just looking for a gathering of Soul Mates, Spirit Sisters or Brothers, and people who **Get Me**.

What Connections are you looking for?

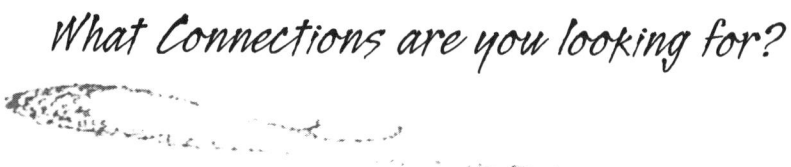

Engage Your Heart

Reflect on the **Heed Your Heart Questions** in this exercise and determine what the important Connections are in your life and how they have influenced you.

Jot your ideas down here:

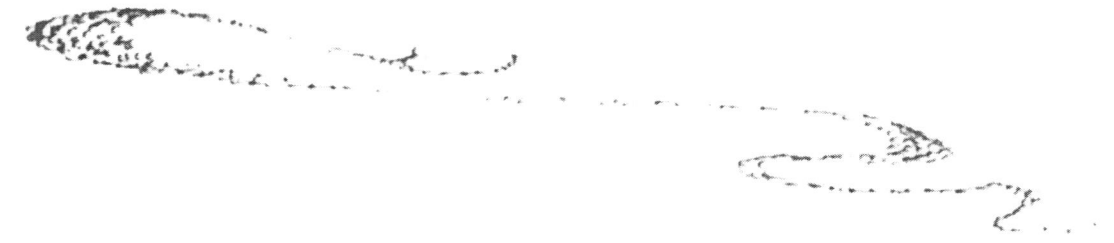

Turn the *Heart Message* *Desires* into actual *Heart Messages* and see if any of them match someone you know.

Example: I am curious about what you are finding delightful these days, because I know the same things will enrich my life.

Write at least one *Heart Message* to acknowledge a person that has been *a Thread that Connects You* **with important aspects of your being.**

Send them your **Heart Message**.

Encouragements From the Heart

Heart Intentions

Create Connections that enrich the world.

Be conscious of who you invite into your Heart.

Intangible Gift

Staying *In Touch* is an *Intangible Gift*.

Bring Along

Your Companionship.

Heart Connection

Be the *Thread* that weaves in and out of your life's tapestry.

Take Aways

Identify the types of Connections you wish to include in your Life.

Careful observation gives us an intimate Connection to our world, both personal and planetary.

Intertwine the threads in your life.

Pass your gratitude along.

Examine the values and beliefs that have endured throughout your life.

Call in.

Creating **Heart Messages** is a process of examining our values and our preferences, of becoming more observant and more articulate in expressing our feelings.

It becomes a practice of reflecting upon the role others have played in our development, and it becomes a way of growing to know ourselves.

"We are the flow; we are the ebb. We are the weavers; we are the web."
                    Shekinah Mountainwater

Align Your Heart

Heart Intentions

Align Your Heart to diffuse, rather than escalate a situation.

Take time to restore yourself.

An *Aligned Heart* brings balance to its Connections by consciously putting others at ease.

It filters the extraneous, in order to restore and recharge on an energetic level.

It will remain suspended in a state of flow.

Its message will promote growth and harmony.

When it occurs, we feel serene.

Discover Ways to Align Your Heart

Occasionally we are all in need of alignment,
physically, emotionally, intellectually, and spiritually.

It is important to take time out of our busy days to check the alignment of our
Hearts and thoughts with the actions and behaviors we exhibit.

A quantum adjustment may be just what is required.

When you *Align Your Heart*, you will discover that you are
in a position to diffuse rather than escalate a situation.

This will allow you to respond to situations with an increasing degree
of compassion, which will build Connections,
which in turn will enhance the quality of your relationships,
which will make you smile,
which will improve your moods,
which will impact your entire existence,
which will…

Well, you get the idea!

Nowhere to go. Nothing to do.

Heart Companion: *Bring Along your Serenity.*

Heart Tales

"Nowhere to go. Nothing to do."

Soothing words filled with possibility, spoken by my yoga teacher.

My imagination takes me to a Secret Garden where my very own sunbeam is awaiting my arrival, where there are no interruptions, no mechanical noises, no everyday stresses, only the whispers of flowers blooming, trees growing and boulders recording history! I love entering this state of flow, although it takes me awhile to quiet the chatter of my thoughts. They continually want to resist the truth of this calming statement. Yet, I am encouraged to insist that for a brief section of time, I actually can create a space where I indeed have **Nowhere to go and Nothing to do**. And insist I must, because every part of my being is cheering me on.

Yes to being restored and rejuvenated!

Yes to stillness!

Yes to serenity.

Yes to thinking **above** the line.

Yes to *Aligning Your Heart.*

Yes to those who help us feel this way.

Heartfelt Connections

You are my Secret Garden.

You let me be myself.
You are the person with whom I am totally relaxed and at ease.
You nourish my soul.

Who is the Secret Garden in your life?

Heed Your Heart Questions

It is highly probable that the person you have identified as your Secret Garden is adept at showing appreciation and encouraging others on a path of self-discovery.

When you are stressed, who is your calming influence?

How do you still your mind in order to integrate your thoughts?

How do you *Align Your Heart*, mind and spirit?

Is your Heart in need of alignment?

Do you need to *Align Your Heart* with someone else's?

Would it make life easier if your **Heart Intention** was harmony?

How do you slow the rush of time?

What circumstances allow you to be reflective?

Where is your Secret Garden?

Blissful Heart Activity

While you are thinking about the answers to the Heed your Heart questions:

Breathe In, and Breathe Out.

Open your mouth and as you exhale, say Ahhhh.

Make it a deep, slow vocalization. If someone overhears you, great! Perhaps it will remind them to bring a moment of serenity into their day.

Do it again, only **LOUDER.**

Set aside three minutes out of each day to BE in stillness.

How can we be so diligent about recharging our cell phones and other electronic devices, and not give our bodies and our minds time to recharge?

We all deserve at least 3 minutes of having: **Nowhere to go and Nothing to do.**

Serene Heart Qualities

Select one of these qualities as your *Intangible Gift*.

Calm
Relaxed
At ease
Be yourself
Loved
Harmonious
Valued
Contented
Rejuvenated
Restored

Peaceful
Grounded
Contemplative
Reflective
Transformative
Still
Integrated
Flexible
Balanced
Intuitive

Heart Messages

Who comes to mind when you read these messages?
These are the people who *Align Your Heart.*
They are your *Secret Garden.*

You have a way of putting me at ease.

Life seems more harmonious when I am around you.

When we are together, I find that I am rejuvenated.

Such a sense of calm comes over me when I'm with you.

I hear your voice saying, **Quiet, quiet, settle down.**

Your soothing words allow me to handle the chaos around me.

When you walk into a room, everyone seems to breathe a sigh of relief.

You have a freshness of spirit that reminds me of the value of considering Karma and the Golden Rule.

Are you the Secret Garden in anyone's life?

For one week, keep track of any Heart Messages that you receive.

Give more to get more.

Engage Your Heart

What do you do to make others feel at ease?

When you are clear regarding your own emotions and feelings, you are able to be more effective in relieving the stress in others.

Secret Garden Cues that are responses worth repeating:

Be patient. **Be** reassuring. **Be** grounded.

Align Your Heart with those you care about.

Diffuse rather than escalate a situation.

Here is one of my most helpful Serene responses:

Sweet Time

When I was working overseas in Singapore, I didn't have a car. In order to make sure that I got to work on time each morning, I scheduled a taxi to pick me up at 6:30 am. The driver was so conscientious, that he kept arriving in front of my house each morning at 6:15. One might expect that I would be pleased by this more than prompt appearance.

Ha!

At that hour of the morning, all I wanted was the opportunity to enjoy a relaxing cup of coffee without the feeling that someone was outside waiting for me.

I became so frustrated that I finally marched out one morning and vocally expressed my agitation.

Fortunately, his response was soothing: "You just take your own *Sweet Time* and don't worry about me. I have to get here this early or I could run into rush hour traffic, which would make me late."

I went back inside and thought about his suggestion to take my own *Sweet Time*. His advice surfaces whenever I feel that urgency to **hurry up** from some compartment of my brain. His wisdom continues to calm me when I impose deadlines on myself.

A certain clarity appears when I contemplate the possibility of taking my own Sweet Time.

Align Your Heart - Engage Your Heart

Identify 3 actions that your *Aligned Heart* could take that would diffuse a stressful situation.

1.

2.

3.

In what ways could you be the *Secret Garden* in someone's life?

Align Your Heart - Engage Your Heart

Create a **Heart Message** for your *Secret Garden*.

What are her/his *Intangible Gifts*?

Use the Serene Heart Quality list or elaborate on the following example for inspiration.

Example:
I am sending you this image of snowflakes falling. I can sense your presence within the calmness.

Align Your Heart - Engage Your Heart

Encouragements From the Heart

Heart Intentions
Align Your Heart to diffuse, rather than escalate a situation.
Take time to restore yourself.

Intangible Gift
All of the *Serene Qualities* are *Intangible Gifts* you can give.

Bring Along
Your *Serenity*.

Heartfelt Connections
Be a *Secret Garden*.

Take Aways
Schedule moments in each day to have: **Nowhere to go and Nothing to do.**
Reflect on your inner world.
Discover the real you and be yourself.
Self-discovery is one of Life's most important finds.
Breathe.
Schedule time for stillness.
Recharge on an energetic level.
Take your own *Sweet Time* whenever you can.
When your mind wanders, follow.
Quantum physics tells us that we are constantly flickering in and out of existence.
How are you feeling?

"Sitting quietly, doing nothing, spring comes, and the grass grows by itself."
Zen proverb

Resilient Heart

Heart Intentions

Activate Your Resilient Heart to cope with adversity and change.

Flow with each new reality.

A *Resilient Heart* embraces Connections by being resourceful and optimistic.
It clicks on an image of the future by setting priorities and defining preferences.
It will bounce back from adversity and change.
Its message will convey compassion and provide comfort.
When it appears, we feel nurtured.

When change appears in our lives, it is a signal to activate our Resilient Heart.

If we don't know where we are going or what lies ahead, yet we are eager to find out, we approach change as an opportunity to explore. We thrive on meeting the challenge ahead by being adaptable and inventive and by heeding our intuition.

On the other hand, when change provokes anxiety or fear, it can become debilitating. We want to cling to what is familiar, including our assumptions, our habits and our routines.

A primary factor in enabling us to react in a resilient manner in the face of unwelcome change, loss or adversity, is the presence of supportive relationships upon which to lean. The beating of our courageous Heart is comforted by the reassurance from others that our resilient spirit possesses an amazing degree of flexibility.

There are times when it becomes critical to examine our priorities and our preferences.

We continually need to differentiate what holds importance for us by making choices that help us to evolve and grow. Perhaps we have made assumptions along the way that did not turn out to be true. We are required to determine what is of most value to us and to make sure our selections support the essence of who we are.

It is crucial to teach each other how to embrace uncertainty by disclosing a way to feel comfortable with ambiguity, and by experimenting with Life's puzzle of contradictions.

Resilience demands that we face an unknown future by flowing with a new reality, because the more we practice resilience, the more resilient we become.

Resilience insists that we be resourceful and determined.

Resilience is an inner knowing that what we need to survive is attainable and that we are supported in our efforts.

It requires a resolve in approach that believes challenges are an everlasting series of occasions for hope.

Will They Have Avocados?

Heart Companion: *Bring Along your Resourcefulness.*

Heart Tales

It was a major life style decision.

She had always lived in California and now she was being asked to move to the Midwest.

Her innermost fears were revealed in one simple question:

Will they have avocados?

The answers she was really seeking were: Will things feel familiar? How many adjustments will I have to make? What unknown changes are coming my way? Will I be lonely? Will I be afraid?

How will the guacamole taste? How will this new life taste?

All of us have experienced times in our lives when we wonder if what our future contains will include the things we hold dear.

Will They Have Avocados?
Is a metaphor about filling the reservoir of what we perceive will be lost, missing or left behind.

It is at these times when we most need reminding that this feeling of facing life's unusual journeys into the unknown will not go on forever, nor will we have to manage all by ourselves.

It is times like these that require us to have a *Resilient Heart*.

Heartfelt Connections

You are my Comfort.

You are the one who helps me to feel supported when life's challenges arise.
You are the person I turn to for reassurance, the one who is always there for me.
You hold open the realm of the unforeseen.

Who do you turn to when you need comforting?

Heed Your Heart Questions

Who do you call for help and assistance when you need the *Intangible Gift* of *Compassion*?

Who knows how to soothe and console you?
Who do you feel empathizes with your circumstances?
Who boosts your morale?
Who can wait patiently while your tears fall?

What could your *Comfort* do to make you feel better?
Listen? Reassure? Show compassion? Take charge? Hold you?
Kiss it and make it better?

What are the consoling words that you wish to hear?
Poor sweet baby.
There, there, everything will be OK.
I'll be right here.
What would a Teddy Bear do?

Is being resourceful one of your *Resilient Heart* Intentions?

How do you seek comfort?
By petting the pooch? Cuddling with something soft (think Teddy Bear)?
Being creative? Looking at photographs? Holding someone's hand?
Listening to music? Going outside? Being in nature? Exercising, dancing?
By reading, doing yoga or meditation?
Eating comfort foods? By talking to yourself or the plants?
By calling a friend? Sleeping? Cleaning house?
By just sitting and letting the wave of discomfort wash over you?

Add your ideas to the list.

Blissful Heart Activity

Look at your hands.

Open your palms.

Close your palms.

Which feels more comfortable?

Sit with your palms in your preferred position for 10 seconds.

Comforting Heart Qualities

Compassionate

Encouraging

Comforting

Consoling

Nurturing

Soothing

Reassuring

Loving

Insightful

Gentle

Secure

Reliable

On my team

In my corner

Heart Messages

Keeping track of Comforting experiences comes in handy when no one but the Teddy Bear is available.

Here are some thoughts to Comfort you:

You are the one I turn to when I need a **Poor Sweet Baby** or someone to say **Don't worry, everything will be just fine.** I always know that together we can find a solution to any dilemma.

Sharing time with you is such an important part of my life. You are part of my foundation. It is as if you wave a magic wand and the world becomes a brighter place.

How wonderful to have you call just to make sure I made it home over the mountain pass. It makes me feel safer knowing that you are checking in with me.

Waking up to the smell of freshly brewed coffee is an exquisite experience. Having you bring me a steaming cup with 3 inch foam on top, while I prop myself up in bed, is beyond divine. Being **stuck in the sheets** for those few extra moments is sheer bliss and is one of the many reasons I love you more each day.

Sometimes I just like to sit and watch the snow melt. I am comfortable doing that with you.

You let me cry and then dry my tears and then make me laugh. *You are...* my *Comfort*.

Through it all you see my inner essence, not my outer mask.

I have learned that when you are down, it is best to make you a cup of tea and answer **Yes Dear**, in a soothing tone.

Engage Your Heart

How has the person you identified as your Comfort helped you to examine your Resilient Heart?

Write a **Heart Message** for that person describing what it meant to you to be able to turn to them for comfort.

Under what circumstances do you most need your *Resilient Heart?*

Encouragements From the Heart

Heart Intentions
Activate Your *Resilient Heart* to cope with adversity and change.
A Resilient Heart flows with each new reality.

Intangible Gift
Your *Compassion*.

Bring Along
Your *Resourcefulness*.

Heartfelt Connection
Be a *Comfort*.

Take Aways
Behave like a Teddy Bear.

Put the one who is your Comfort at the top of your contact list.

Be flexible.

Bounce back.

Clarify your preferences and examine your priorities.

Believe in limitless possibilities and as many new beginnings as you need.

Music is comforting. **Be Great** for the length of one song.

Show up and be soothing.

If you permit your attitude to alter its stance on a position, you can transform your life in a second.

Assess what is happening as it comes along. Build on what is working and let go of the rest.

Repair the world that is within your reach.

Have a cup of tea and contemplate the **Heart Messages** you have received.

"Sometimes the only available transportation is a leap of faith."
                                                    Margaret Shepherd

Expand Your Heart

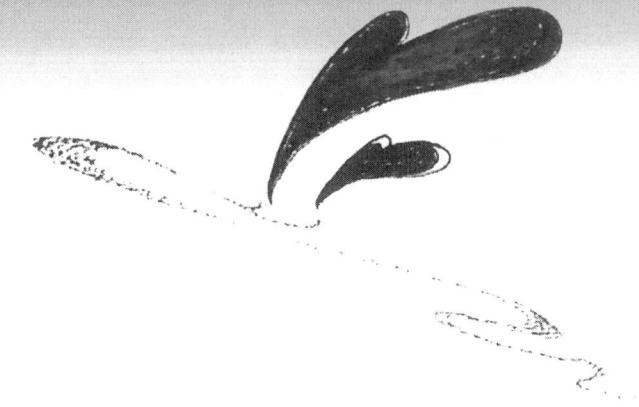

Heart Intentions

Expand your Heart to create more space for who and what you value.

Wake Up! Seek Fulfillment.

An *Expanded Heart* attracts Connections by being alert and aware.

Its vision encompasses a worldview.

It will continually evolve.

Its message will be one of abundance and amazement.

When we encounter it, we feel energized.

Tick Tock, the Clock

Since one way to expand our vision of time is by fostering long lived ways of thinking, I am trying to think of my own existence in more expansive terms. When I was 27, I attended a workshop in which each participant was asked to draw a simple time line with the date of their birth on one end and the year they thought they would die on the other end of the continuum. I put 80 years old as my life expectancy.

I have changed my mind.

Eighty seems a lot closer than it did at 27. I have drawn a longer line on my original paper, which, by the way, was amazingly easy to do. This extended line allows for more possibilities and eliminates any dread that time may be running out sooner than I expected. It broadens my vision. It breathes more energy into what the future may hold and it revitalizes my belief that I still have plenty of time to anticipate and enjoy the experiences that await me.

Access the *Intangible Gift* of *Awareness* and begin by surrounding yourself with people who have an affirming vision for the future. Hold positive expectations of your own existence.

Give more latitude and longitude to those that share different worldviews by momentarily putting aside your conclusions. Yes, by all means, live in the Now, but consider making it a Long Now.

And no doubt the future will unfold,
in some mysterious way that we can't even imagine,
but in a way that our collective preferences have influenced.

My Cells are Ringing

Heart Companion: Bring Along your Amazement at being alive.

Heart Tales

When the New Year's moon is full, I have a ritual of reflecting on what has attracted my attention in the year gone by. It is a time to recognize the enthusiasms that have awakened in me.

Most recently, I have been drawn to groupings of floating circles within circles, in all shapes and sizes. Not knowing what to make of these images, I cut out pictures and photos of them and kept them in a box, until one day I started reading a book on biology.

Did YOU know that we have over 50 trillion cells? It was a revelation to me.

I became so intrigued, that I finally studied how our cells function. Presumably this was taught in 10th grade biology class, but at fifteen I was unaware of the existence of a cellular level within me.

Visualizing my cells makes me appreciate the wonder of my outside in and my inside out.

I have come to the realization that the strange circles I collected represent the cells of my being.

If I listen carefully, I think that I can hear their particular ring tones.

"I awaken my Heart each day attuned to the hum of Aliveness, and to the awareness of my interior landscape.

Heartfelt Connections

You are my Awakening Rhythm.

You energize me with your laughter, your optimism and your enthusiasm.
You are the one who motivates me to get up and get going.

Who makes you feel more aware and alive?

Heed Your Heart Questions

When I am having difficulty articulating a particular quality I want to emphasize about a person, I think of words beginning with the letters of the alphabet. You can do this by selecting a letter and listing the words that come forward. Use this technique to vary your vocabulary.

Expand Your Heart with the **Intention** of creating a space for *All the A's*.

Here is a list of *All A's* for you to consider:

Alert, Alive, Awake, Aspire, Aware, Anticipation, Acknowledge, Ask, Amplify, Amaze, Animate, Attend, Attune, Attention, Accept, Appreciate, Abundance, Available & Action.

What heightens your *awareness*?

What *actions* do you take to make yourself *available* to learning and growing?

What is *awakening* in you?

What do you want to *amplify*?

What attracts your *attention*?

When do you feel the most *alert* and *alive*?

What *amazes* you?

What are you *anticipating*?

What *aspirations* do you have?

What types of *abundance* are you attracting?

What do you *appreciate* about your *Awakening Rhythm*?

Blissful Heart Activity

Stretch your arms out like airplane wings, as wide as they will go.

Get Long!

Expand your Heart and your Thinking.

Expansive Heart Qualities

Alive
Conscious
Enlightened
Energetic
Joyful
Uplifted *Joie de Vie*
Inspired *Overflowing*
Expressive *Fountaining*
Infectious *Happy*
Upbeat *Sensuous*
Animated
Playful
Creative/Imaginative
Visionary
Fresh Perspectives

Heart Messages

These Heart Messages describe someone who is an Awakening Rhythm, and incorporate some of the All A's to Amaze you.

We are *attuned* to the same rhythms. Our strides move at the same pace when we are walking. We intuitively know each other's movements before they happen.

The same shapes, the same colors and the same beauty in nature capture our *attention*. Our enthusiasms juggle for position.

It is such a delight to be around you, because you make me feel so *alive*.

I always *anticipate* our times together, because I know that your laughter will lift my spirits.

I am *alert* to a well of energy rising within me when we collaborate on projects.

Isn't it fascinating how we *amplify* our thinking by having the same thoughts at the same time?

Envision creating messages for the people who Expand Your Heart.

I love being in your presence! I find your ideas and conversations so uplifting, so filled with enthusiasm and energy. I just thought you should know what a positive impact you have. It is contagious!

Thank you for introducing me to a new creative process. I would not have thought to select words for a creative composition based on their color and font. How exciting it is to think outside the box, when a friend is there to expand your thinking.

You radiate a joie de vivre that is infectious.

You have retained a youthful enthusiasm, which makes you ageless.

Engage Your Heart

Select three people who *Expand Your Heart* and identify their passions, enthusiasms, and/or fascinations.

1.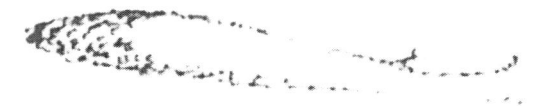

2.

3.

Create a **Heart Message** that acknowledges what amazes you about the people you have chosen. Is it something you share in common?

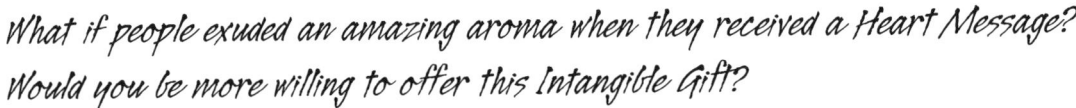

Explain how each person *enhances* your *excitement*.
(*See, you can play with any letter*)

What if people exuded an amazing aroma when they received a Heart Message?
Would you be more willing to offer this Intangible Gift?

Incorporate the ideas expressed in the **Expansive Qualities** into a **Heart Message** for the people who inspire you to discover new ways of seeing the world.

Encouragements From the Heart

Heart Intentions
Expand Your Heart to create space for who and what you value.

Fill the open spaces with **All A's**.

Alert, Alive, Awake, Aspire, Aware, Anticipation, Acknowledge, Ask, Amplify, Amaze, Animate, Attend, Attune, Attention, Accept, Appreciate & Abundance.

Seek Fulfillment.

Intangible Gift
Express your gratitude for the *Intangible Gift* of *Awareness*.

Bring Along
Your *Amazement*.

Heart Connection
Be an *Awakening Rhythm*.

Take Aways
Be *Attuned* to the song your cells are singing.

Allow your Heart to be *Amazed*.

Follow your inner rhythms.

Be *Aware* before you do anything else. Chronicle your *Awareness*.

Look for new modes of expression. *Attend* to the **All A's**.

Act old later and be *Alive* now.

Keep track of what inspires you.

Extend your worldview. Envision your existence. Evolve. Make it a **Long Now**.

Step out of your belief system for the length of a conversation.

Using any of the **All A's**, add your own *Take Aways* from this segment.

"Life is change. Growth is optional. Choose wisely."
 Karen Kaiser Clark

Receptive Heart

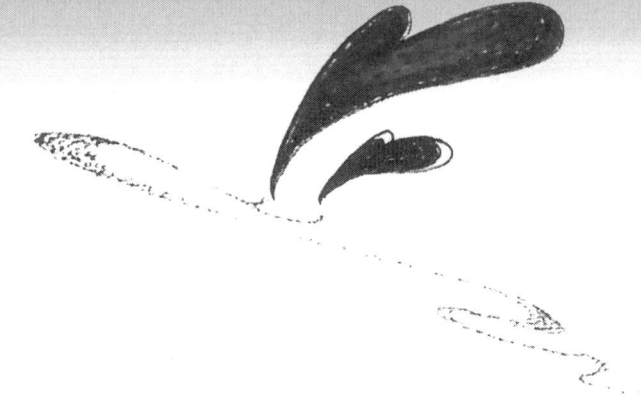

Heart Intentions

A Receptive Heart helps others find their voice.

Receptive Hearts listen between the lines.

A *Receptive Heart* cements Connections by offering its full attention.
It zooms in on mindfulness and is acutely aware of what is happening in the moment.
It will admit other points of view.
Its message will be non-judgmental.
When it approaches us, we feel accepted.

A Bit Odd

Do you have an eccentric relative residing in your family tree?
We did. She often struck us as *A Bit Odd*.

Although she is no longer in this physical realm, her stories and her way of viewing Life lives on in family gatherings. Her viewpoints were based in colonialism and would not be at all politically correct in today's world. She had a way of expressing her opinions that went straight to the point. Although she knew how to be very proper, she never allowed this expectation to restrain her. Her independent spirit and bohemian ways made her unique in her time. She was difficult to please, not because she was contrary, but because she had seen and done so much that it took a lot to astound her. As I said, we thought she was eccentric. I won't disclose family secrets, but trust me, she was. Nevertheless, she made a deep impression upon me.

Here is an anecdote from a portion of one evening we spent together.

My husband and I wanted to make her visit to see us memorable, so we decided to take her out to dinner upon her arrival. Prior to being seated at the table, she and I both stopped at the restroom. As we were re-applying our lipstick and combing our hair, she looked at me in the mirror and said: *"I finally understand why you two get along so well. It is because you are both A Bit Odd."*

I was momentarily taken aback, but I decided to approach her remark with a *Receptive Heart*. Eccentric can be good, right? So I replied, "Well, thank you. We think you are *A Bit Odd* too, and that is why we love you."

Her already erect posture grew an inch, and she retorted, "**Harrumph**, there is nothing the *least Bit Odd* about me."

So keep in mind, as you go out into the real world with your **Heart Messages**, not everyone will be instantly receptive. They may think you too are *A Bit Odd* for expressing your thoughts in such a genuine manner. Some people may initially be a little embarrassed or uncomfortable. Their reaction might catch you off guard. Not everyone will respond in kind.

Be assured that whatever their immediate response to you may be, eventually your efforts will please them. Perhaps your words will echo in their ears as they get ready for bed and they will fall asleep with a smile on their face. Perhaps they will awaken with your **Heart Message** inscribed on their now more *Receptive Heart*.

Perhaps they too will find joy in being *A Bit Odd* and the social environment we inhabit will evolve into a more gentle atmosphere, which will allow us all to prosper.

All Ears

Heart Companion: *Bring Along your Attention.*

Heart Tales

We had just managed the timing of a fascinating new rhythm, when the leader of our drumming circle, a music teacher, unexpectedly asked us to lend our individual voices to the beat. Anything resembling music swiftly fell apart. After several failed attempts, we put down our drums in frustration.

"Listen," she said, "We all have A Voice that is unique in the Universe. When you die, that sound, the sound of your voice, will never exist again. Your voice is one of your most identifying signatures, so let yourself be known."

The impact of her words made me realize that each of us deserves to be heard, pitch perfect or not.

We also need a *Sounding Board* who can hear our Voices between the lines.

Words flow out of our mouths that are hidden from view until we permit our thoughts to speak out loud. Somehow, by hearing our own ideas reach the ears of someone else, clarity emerges in our minds. Our intuition takes center stage and realization dawns on us. The *Intangible Gift* of *Tenderness* enters the internal and external conversation.

This is the world of **All Ears**.

When you hear the word listen, do you translate it to Shut Up? Shut Up implies that you also shut down. This is the opposite of **All Ears**.

A completely focused attention on what is being said is required when you are **All Ears**. That is how you are able to hear the voices between the lines. One of the purposes of a *Sounding Board* is to project the sound. As you become adept at being **All Ears**, your noiseless attention will project the speaker's thoughts and allow them to hear their own inner voice, a truly unique sound in the Universe.

Heartfelt Connections

You are my Sounding Board.

I trust your advice;
I rely on you for clarification & for reassurance.
You listen between the lines;
You hear what I mean, regardless of what I say.
You are the one who helps me find my Voice.

Who Pays Attention when you wish to be heard?

Heed Your Heart Questions

Being a *Sounding Board* is one of the most critical roles we can play for one another.

"Listen," sounds so easy, yet listening is an art that is astoundingly difficult to perfect. Often our natural tendency is to offer advice. Our desire to help others benefit from our experience becomes overwhelming. Judgment nudges and shoves its way to the surface, despite our best intentions. Perhaps we are so used to being the one in control, the one who fixes things, The Voice, that we find it next to impossible to be a *Sounding Board*. When this occurs, we deprive others of the opportunity to hear their thoughts spoken aloud.

Enjoying the long, slow pauses, in which thoughts are processed, means waiting to be invited to speak. You will recognize the signal. It may be a nod, a glance, or a request. Then is the time to paraphrase back what you have heard, to reinforce what rings true, to ask questions that will guide others to their own conclusions.

Would hearing, "I'm *All Ears*," sound good to you?

In what ways do you listen to your heart?

Whisper the answer.

What ideas or concerns would you like to bounce off your *Sounding Board*?

How comfortable are you with Pauses?

When someone says Listen, do you hear Shut Up?
When someone says Shut Up, do you hear Listen?

Tune Your *Receptive Heart* **Intentions** to hear between the lines.

Can you be *All Ears*?

How does Bringing Along your Attention improve your Connections?

Blissful Heart Activity

Rub your ear lobes and roar like a lion.

What?
Yes, it is silly.

Did you get anyone's Attention?

Receptive Heart Qualities

Receptive
Non-judgmental
Accepts
Listens
Clarifies
Advises
Reinforces
Questions
Pays attention
Respects
Discerning
Sees the big picture
Provides perspective
Reality Check

Heart Messages

Here are some Heart Messages intended for a *Sounding Board* who listens with a *Receptive Heart* and actually hears what is said.

You ask just the right questions to put me in touch with my own inner wisdom.

It really helps to have someone who doesn't interrupt my train of thought when I'm trying to clarify my thinking.

If our conversation veers off on a tangent, I know you will bring us back to the topic at hand.

When I share my concerns with you, I really appreciate that you are non-judgmental, because I don't have to censor what I share.

You are the one I turn to when I need to bounce an idea off someone whose advice I trust.

We recognize one another by the language we use. I know that you understand the feelings behind what I say.

I admire the way that you can differentiate between a conversation, a discussion and those times when I just need someone to listen. You are so easy to talk to.

If you let me know that you need a *Sounding Board*, I will do my best to be **All Ears**.

"No one will listen to us unless we listen to ourselves."
Marianne Williamson

Engage Your Heart

What can your Sounding Board say or do that would make you feel as if you were really being heard?

Make your answer a **Heart Message** and share their *Intangible Gifts* with them.
Try to incorporate the *Receptive Heart* **Qualities**.

Encouragements From the Heart

Heart Intentions
Listen between the lines with your *Receptive Heart*.
Help others to find their voice.

Intangible Gift
Your *Tenderness*.

Bring Along
Your *Attention*!

Heartfelt Connection
Be a *Sounding Board*.

Take Aways
Practice being **All Ears**.

We hear hundreds of messages a day. Tune in to the ones that require your *Receptive Heart*.

Sounding Boards are invaluable and need to be told how much they mean to us.

Useful thoughts leave us feeling steady and clear, and move us forward.

Being *A Bit Odd* may be the only way to make the world a better place.

Remember, everyone has his/her own story that they need someone to hear.

People do what they have to do in order to survive on the inside.

Listen to your own Heart.

Offer advice only if it is requested.

Defer judgement.

"Don't believe everything you think."
                    Eckhart Tolle

Bold Heart

Heart Intentions

Summon your Bold Heart when Adventure calls.

Raise vibrations. Explore new experiences.

A *Bold Heart* explores Connections by initiating adventures.
It concentrates on what is happening outside the comfort zone.
It will seek out new experiences.
Its message will be one of anticipation and daring.
When we discover it, we feel exhilarated.

A Bold Heart thrives, not just survives.

If you encounter times when your best efforts seem thwarted and you feel as if you are just surviving instead of thriving, look around and see what is beckoning you.

Is it an Adventure? Is it a spontaneous impulse? Is it trying something new, even if it makes you feel a little anxious?

When you introduce the unexpected and the unpredictable into your routine in the form of an Adventure, you heighten your awareness by requiring your senses to be more alert.

When you approach new experiences with an adventuresome spirit, it allows you to cross the threshold that leads to a questing Heart. It is in this space that you can more fully appreciate the desirable state of awareness we call existence. If you set your curiosity and imagination into motion, an exploration is launched.

Setting out on adventures is one of the ways in which you can express your independence. As you become more aware of your capabilities, you will increase the feeling of accomplishment that boosts your confidence, which could result in your next move being even bolder.

It is astonishing to discover the doors that will open
for those who possess a *Bold Heart*.

Look behind you.

Look up and down.

Look to your left. Look to your right.

You never know when *Adventure* will be waiting for you.

Perhaps an *Adventure* is standing by your side right now

and all you have to do is take its hand.

Share a **Heart Tale** *about an Adventure you have had!*

Six Bucks and a Kiss on the Cheek

Heart Companion: *Bring Along your Curiosity.*

Heart Tales

It started with a quest for a Bedouin scarf.

Wandering through a market area in North Africa during a more innocent time, I happened upon a Bedouin nomad selling jewelry that was artfully displayed upon a blanket. Curious, I bent down to examine a necklace in a beautiful shade of blue and adorned with Bedouin silver (recycled material from aluminum cans). He instantly began to bargain. I explained that although the necklace was pretty, I really wanted to locate one of the 9 foot blue Bedouin scarves that have been worn throughout history to protect the head and face against the desert elements of sand, wind and sun.

Ignoring my request, his focus continued to be the necklace. His first offer was," For you, only $60".

I did not need the necklace, so I responded with a price I presumed would end the negotiations. "Six dollars." Amazingly, instead of being insulted, he became more insistent. There was nothing left for me to do but walk away. In parting, I did tell him, "If you can find the scarf, I will buy it from you".

Later that afternoon, in a completely different section of the city, the Bedouin man appeared at my side. "Come with me to my sisters," he said. "They have the scarf." After some deliberations, and many assurances, we went to visit the sisters. These two beautiful young women did indeed have exactly the scarf for which I had been searching. They were so engaging, that I asked for them to show me how to wrap it around my head, which then led to a lesson in eye makeup, including outlining my eyes in kohl and shadows. One look in their hand mirror showed me that the transformation from blonde and wholesome to exotic and tribal had been successful. Now it was time for photos. Or so I thought.

But wait.

The blue necklace has appeared again, dangling between the fingers of the Bedouin man.

"How it compliments the scarf. How it makes your eyes sparkle."

Their flattery succeeded. It was the perfect accessory.

"How much will you pay?" he asked.

"Your asking price for the scarf and $6.00 for the necklace", I replied.

To my amazement he countered with, "OK, six dollars and a kiss."
This exchange elicited peals of laughter from the sisters.

"**Six bucks and a kiss on the cheek,**" I replied, to which everyone applauded and agreed.

Feeling adventuresome is so important to me. Although I live in a beautiful area, frequent daydreams about exotic places flutter through my thoughts. My motto for years has been **Expect the Unexpected**. I have learned that we can sometimes orchestrate our adventures in travel and in life, but at other times, they catch us by surprise.

They can become unexpected delights.

This interaction with a nomadic culture turned out to be one of my most cherished memories.

I still have the scarf and the necklace.

Over a decade later, seeing either purchase floods me with a feeling of gratitude and appreciation for this unexpected adventure that my Bold Heart undertook.

Bold Heart - *Heart Tales*

Heartfelt Connections

You are the Adventure in my Routine.

You energize me.
You help set aside my inhibitions.
You are an unexpected delight.
You create a space for me to be spontaneous.

Who brings Adventure into your everyday life?

Heed Your Heart Questions

What if you changed one thing in your routine?

Would that be an Adventure?

What if you made faces at the dinner table?

What if you danced while doing the dishes?

What if you tickled someone while they were brushing their teeth?

Aren't you thrilled when everything falls into place and you feel as if you are flowing effortlessly in the right direction?

What defines an *Adventure* for you?

What gives you a feeling of exhilaration?

Is it your *Bold Heart* **Intention** to create meaningful experiences?

On a scale of 1 to 5, with 5 being the highest degree, how Adventuresome are you?

Blissful Heart Activity

What Adventure would you like to be up to right now?

Can you make a version of this happen in the real world?

Plan an *Adventure* that you can do in the next 24 hours.

Give someone an unexpected kiss on the cheek.

Open your eyes and mouth wide in surprise.

Bold Heart Qualities

Adventurous
Daring
Exciting
Exhilarating
Thrilling
Animated
Courageous
Humorous
Uninhibited
Be myself
Playful
Mischievous
Spontaneous
Impetuous
Unpredictable

Heart Messages

Travel, Travel, Travel

That is my fascination. There was a time in my life when I believed that I had to go far afield to have an adventure. If I didn't take a year off and travel around the world visiting third world cultures or go trekking in the Himalayas, it didn't count as an adventure. Perhaps I am wiser, because I have come to realize that adventures can occur close to home as well.

Here are some everyday adventures that happened to me, along with the Bold Heart Messages that I created to celebrate them.

How did you know that I wanted to invite more spontaneity into my everyday life? I can't think of a better example than chasing rainbows with you this afternoon. Capturing such fleeting moments is what life is all about. Never mind about the screeching of tires as we pulled off the interstate. Others may have passed up the opportunity and missed the thrill of seeing prisms in the sky. I am so glad I was along for the ride.

Who else would call at 8:30 at night and ask if they could deliver a 'warm from the oven' pear tart? Just you. I am still smacking my lips.

What a wonder!
I laughed at the sight of such an unusual, but beautiful vegetable sitting on my doorstep.
I know you left it.
I've never seen it before.
Where is it from?
What is it called?
I am so lucky to have you to bring me unexpected delights.

Magical events always manifest themselves when we are together.

Engage Your Heart

Hopefully your Sense of Adventure is alive and well.

Think of an adventure that you shared with someone or an adventure that you enjoyed by yourself.

What elements were present that identified these events as adventures?

Express your desire to incorporate more adventure into your life by creating a *Bold Heart* **Message**.

What *Intangible Gifts* will you need to *Bring Along*?

Focus on any of the *Exploring Qualities*.

Encouragements From the Heart

Heart Intentions
Summon your *Bold Heart* when *Adventure* calls.
Raise vibrations. Explore new experiences.

Intangible Gift
Your *Anticipation*.

Bring Along
Your *Curiosity*.

Heartfelt Connection
Be the *Adventure*.

Take Aways
Transform your routine into an adventure.

Enjoy the Anticipation.

Seek unexpected delights.

Follow your impulse to be adventuresome.

Take a chance.

Change your routine.

Be the surprise.

Pass your Gratitude along.

Act spontaneously.

Thrive, don't just survive.

Initiate Adventures.

If we don't change the direction we are headed, we will end up where we are going.
Chinese Proverb

"Act boldly and unseen forces will come to your aid."
Dorothy Brande

Identify at least one milestone for each decade of your life.

Circle the milestones or decisions that have required a *Bold Heart*.

My motto is:
"If you have something to look forward to each day,
life will be an Adventure."
Make sure that you offer yourself the *Intangible Gift* of *Anticipation*
by designing something to look forward to.

Is there anything that you currently desire that
will call for you to access your *Bold Heart?*

Guiding Heart

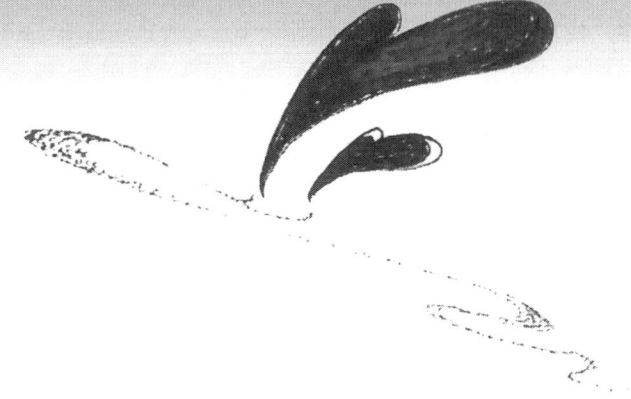

Heart Intentions

A Guiding Heart illuminates the way.

Be the Glow.

A *Guiding Heart* encourages Connections by sharing the wisdom of experience.

It frames its view with protective charms.

It will illuminate the way for us to choose or reject.

Its message is full of concern and direction.

When we accept its intention, we feel treasured.

Kindly Light

Perhaps you have heard that the *Kindly Light*, one of the most legendary Bristol Channel Pilot Cutters, has been restored to her original glory.

Kindly Light, taken from the poem "Pillar of Clouds", is a most perfect name for this class of sailboat.

The Pilot Cutter's function is to transport the pilot to board an incoming ship in need of being guided into port. These skillful pilots have steered many a ship to safety through the difficult tidal waters of the River Severn.

We too are sometimes in need of being transported by a Kindly Light, especially if we are entering into uncharted waters or set adrift amid the storms of Life. We all want to feel assured that the forces who lead us will do so with a Kindly Light.

What compels us to come to the assistance of one another in a time of need?

It is a desire to keep someone out of harms way, to help her/him avoid the pitfalls of life by guiding them through the obstacles and onto the safer pathways of exploration. It is an urge to set up protective boundaries, so that others will not be exposed to pain and suffering. It is a longing to be of service in times of need.

It is finding that fine line between caring and controlling.

It is that Kindly Light that emanates from within our *Guiding Heart*, whose radiance shines for all to see.

To paraphrase James Thurber,

Be the glow that illuminates, not the glare that obscures.

"Kindly Light, amid the encircling gloom, lead Thou me on!
The night is dark and I am far from home…"
John Henry Newman

Watch Your Hair, Lady

Heart Companion: *Bring Along your Inner Compass.*

Heart Tales

At first, this idiomatic American phrase, spoken by a very young girl who was guiding me into the souks of Marrakesh, sounded foreign to my ears.

Watch Your Hair, Lady? Surely she meant, **Watch Your Head**. Yet I knew what she wanted me to do, so I ducked. I wound my way, bent at the knees, through a labyrinth of alleyways, mindful of my hair.

Since then, I hear her words whenever I feel concern for another's or my own safety. I can sense her *Guiding Heart*. I like watching my hair and not just my head, because it provides another level of protection and prevention before anything unpleasant can occur. I still remember the feeling of watching my hair as I successfully avoided bumping my head.

What if we were taught to **Watch Our Hair** and not our head?
Would our lives feel more secure?

Think of how often you've been told: **Don't do this or don't do that**. Even though we know the person admonishing us is trying to protect us or is trying to safeguard the rights of others, usually our ears filter the **Don't** part and the outcome is the opposite of what was intended. That is why a version of **Watch Your Hair, Lady** seems to resonate with me.

Have a safe journey, Take care, Look both ways.
These all give clear direction about what **TO** do and provide us with a little blessing.

The Do's are more empowering and less full of fear than the Don'ts.

Heartfelt Connections

You are my Shining Light.

*You assist me in finding my way, staying on my path, enjoying the journey.
You look out for me by acting as my guide and my guardian.
Your Connection to a higher realm has guided me many times.*

Who watches out for you?

Heed Your Heart Questions

What makes you feel secure?

Is it having a feeling of abundance?

Is it having enough cash flow to pay the bills?

Is it the sound of laughter?

Is it being in sync with a loved one?

Is it an adoring look?

Is it a message to keep in touch?

Is it someone to hold your hand?

Is it having something to look forward to?

Is it finding your own way by yourself
and the inner confidence that comes with the challenges?

Is it a bulletproof vest?

Is it a prayer or a belief that you are supported?

Is it being content with what you have?

Imagine that your *Guiding Heart* **Intention** is to *Be the Glow*.

What other possibilities can you think of?

Tell someone who needs to know what your answers are.

Blissful Heart Activity

*Try saying, "Watch Your Hair!"
in your outside voice.*
(With Volume)

Count how many times in one day you encounter the word *Don't*.

Change *Don't* to *Do*.

Guiding Heart Qualities

Caring

Shows me the way

Steers me in the direction I need to go

Protective

Concerned

Watches out for me

Got my back

Sees consequences

Considerate

Thoughtful

Guides

Leads

Devoted

Patient

Heart Messages

Watercolor Edges

Lost luggage on an international arrival is not usually something I consider a blessing, but in this case it was. I arrived in Venice with no guidebook, no hat and no change of clothes. Determined not to let the fact that I also had no idea where I was going ruin my visit, I bought a gondolier straw hat and a bottle of fizzante water and set off on foot. August heat steered me to a line of shady trees near the waterfront, where I was delighted to discover a series of watercolor paintings on display along the canal pathway. As I strolled slowly past, the artist pointed to one of the paintings and then to a structure near St. Mark's square. This one is of the Bridge of Sighs, he explained.

I was hooked.

Time melted as I surveyed the architecture of Venice through his watercolor eyes. Each time we viewed a picture, the artist pointed out the silhouette of the building he had painted, either on the skyline or on a map.

How fortunate it was that my luggage had been delayed.

He became my Shining Light in a shimmering city.

Finally, I wandered along, only to realize that I always seemed to know where I was, as well as where I was headed. The only explanation for my incredible inner compass was that I had traced the watercolor edges of the city and my *Guide* had been the artist who sold me the Bridge of Sighs.

These messages are designed for the people who help to guide us along life's journey or give us directions to the places we want to go.

They are the *Shining Lights* who offer their thoughtfulness and advice and who speak little blessings on our behalf. They are the ones who look out for us. They may also turn out to be the Bossy Butts. You know the ones who admonish you to **Be careful** and are always checking up on you. If you listen with **All Ears**, you will know that what they may be expressing is their care and concern.

Accept their *Guiding Heart* **with your** *Caring Heart.*

When you double check on me, it used to feel like you didn't trust my capabilities or have confidence in my judgment. I have come to understand that you are watching out for me.

You project a certainty in your stride and an air of integrity that makes people want to confide in you, to seek your advice and opinion. I would follow you anywhere.

I marvel at the accumulation of the many small, caring acts that you perform and how they make my job so much easier.

I know you have my best interests at heart.

I can count on you to steer me in the right direction, which enables me to feel more self-assured.

Knowing that you've got my back allows me to be braver.

You keep me from going off track.

Caring Heart - **Heart Messages**

Engage Your Heart

Consider a time when your Shining Light has looked out for you or showed you the way. How did it make you feel?

Write at least 5 feelings here:

1.

2.

3.

4.

5.

Caring Heart - **Engage Your Heart**

Engage Your Heart

Create a Guiding Heart Message for your Shining Light and share your feelings.

Create a Heartfelt Connection for someone you know:

You are...

Caring Heart - Engage Your Heart

Encouragements From the Heart

Heart Intentions
A *Guiding Heart* illuminates the way.
Be the Glow.

Intangible Gift
Your *Thoughtfulness* and *Concern*.

Bring Along
Your *Inner Compass*.

Heartfelt Connection
Be the *Shining Light*.

Take Aways
Watch your hair.
Tap into a feeling of security, regardless of what the consumer confidence index shows.
Think of warnings, orders, directions and admonishments, as protections.
Ask for help!
Help others find their bearings.
Reach out.
Share your wisdom.
Encourage others on their journey.
Consider the consequences.
Give others a chance to find their own way, unless they are in danger.
Locate your True North, that inner space where you can always find your bearings.

"When things go wrong, don't go with them."
Elvis Presley

Heart Prism

A Prism disperses light.

If you create a Heart Prism,
the colors emanating from the people who are close to you
can influence how much light shines in your world.

Heart Prisms can be very intriguing.

The people who compose my life often appear as mental images in their own unique colors. They are all part of my *Heart Prism*.

In this colorful Universe that I envision, the colors of people's *Intangible Gifts* may vary, but the essence of who they are tends to remain the same.

What may alter are the hues and shades, tones and contrasts. Being aware of their vibrancy or shading also helps me respond to them with my own color spectrum. If they appear as a primary color, I can choose to enhance my pastel palette with a more vibrant tone. Or, if I am vivid and they are subdued in color, perhaps they will brighten up around me. Who knows? Anything can happen when you let your imagination take hold.

What section of the color quadrant describes you?
Is it the Blue/Green, the Red/Orange? The Yellow/Violet?

**Do their colors compliment yours? What if they clash?
Can you modify your color to be more compatible?**

What color am I?
I Am Blue. (Usually periwinkle)
I am blue, flowing, floating, smiling, refreshing, sparkling, deep, full of clarity, revealing surprises beneath my surface, expansive, soothing, reflecting and calm.

On the other hand, if you are rain slicker yellow, I want to be turquoise blue.
I Am Turquoise.
Hear me chant. Follow the beat of my drum.
I will lead you to where the fireflies blink, where the bonfires flame, and where the Northern Lights dance. Moonbeams make me laugh. I mark time by what I was doing on the full moon. Let's go hiking.

Could this be poetry? Pretend it is.

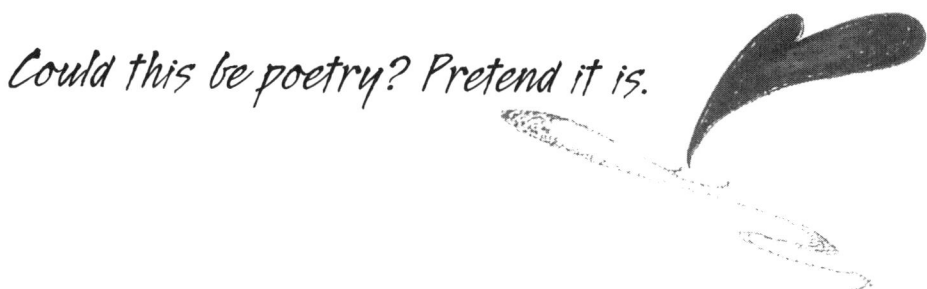

Writing *You Are So You!* **The Path to Uplifting Hearts**,
has afforded me an opportunity to collect
some of my favorite anecdotes and turn them into **Heart Tales**.

It has given me a chance to gather meaningful experiences and insights
and convey the impact they have made on my life to the people who have
shared their wisdom and their joy with me.

My feelings and interpretations are contained within the pages,
inspired by the thoughtfulness and actions of others.

I have felt the electricity of identifying and of giving my own *Intangible Gifts* and I have
discovered the delight of *Bringing Along* the various companions mentioned in each chapter.

I too have experimented with the **Heart Intentions** and
noted the Power each one possesses, when I act from my Heart.

*It is my sincere hope that by giving Intangible Gifts
and by extending Heart Messages
filled with positive feedback and observations,
a Heart Space of sensitivity will emerge in your world
and
the barrier of walls that exists among humankind will collapse.*

Here is your opportunity to revisit the multifaceted Heart Prisms comprising this book.

Determine which areas are ones that you might want to focus upon or have echo in your thoughts.

Heart Intentions

You have encountered various kinds of Hearts in real life and within the covers of this book. Select from the Collection of **Heart Intentions** the ones that best serve you.

Prepare Your Heart for Whatever May Come Your Way.

Follow Your Heart to Discover What Awaits You.

Open Your Heart to Loving deeply, feeling deeply. Be Open to a new way of seeing.

Reveal Your Heart to Those You Cherish and Trust. Unveil Your Hopes and Dreams.

A *Believing Heart* Highlights for Others the Best Versions of Themselves.
Applaud the Efforts of Those You Believe In.

Show Your *Adoring Heart* to the People You Love.
Extend Your Respect, Recognition, and Approval.

Share the Contents of your *Remembering Heart*. Be a Reminder.

A *Connecting Heart* Creates Connections that Enrich the World.
Be Aware of Who and What You Invite into Your Heart

Align Your Heart to Diffuse, rather than Escalate a Situation. Take Time to Restore Yourself.

Activate your *Resilient Heart* to Cope with Change. Flow with Each New Reality.

Expand Your Heart to Create More Space for Who and What You Value. Seek Fulfillment.

A *Receptive Heart* Helps Others to Find Their Voice. *Receptive Hearts* Listen Between the Lines.

Summon Your *Bold Heart* when Adventure calls. Raise Vibrations. Explore New Experiences.

A *Guiding Heart* Illuminates the Way. Be the Glow!

Bring Along Your Companions

These Companions are also *Intangible Gifts* that will enable you to build your Connections with others, as well as yourself. Invite these Companions to accompany you to any engagement or for any occasion. Feel free to *Bring Along* any other companions that enrich your existence and aid in your growth. Find a way to *Bring Along* your companions when you encounter people with whom you want to connect.

Bring Along

Your Smile
Your Confidence
Limitless Possibilities
Your Approval
Your Heart Memories
Your Companionship
Your Serenity
Your Resourcefulness
Your Amazement at Being Alive
Your Attention
Your Curiosity
Your Inner Compass

Intangible Gifts

Your Greeting
Your Enthusiasm
Your Inner Beauty
Super Powers
Marks you have left
Staying in Touch
Serene Qualities
Your Compassion
Awareness
Tenderness
Your Anticipation
Your Thoughtfulness and Concern

Heart Tales

Tell your own **Heart Tales**. They can be compelling **Heart Messages**.

Heartfelt Connections

Reflect back on your **Heartfelt Connections**.

Throughout the book you have identified the people who have played a role in your well being by matching individuals who have made a lasting difference in your life to the **Heartfelt Connections**.

Review the people you have chosen to complete the sentences *You are* …

Who repeatedly showed up in your thoughts?

Who was missing that you might have expected to be present?

What role do they play in your life?

Create you own *You are*… just for them.

What role do you play in the lives of others?

How do you fulfill these needs for yourself?

Approach your relationships with the intention of **Being** the most effective *You are*… in any given circumstance. Add to your repertoire of ways in which to engage with others.
Each *You are* … will bring forth a different response.

You are…

> the Gentle Eyes that Welcome Me.
> the "Yes" in my hesitation.
> my Reflecting Mirror.
> the Scolding Look I Pay Attention to.
> my Then and my Now.
> the Thread that Connects our Hearts.
> my Secret Garden.
> my Comfort.
> my Awakening Rhythm.
> my Sounding Board.
> the Adventure in my Routine.
> my Shining Light.

Heed Your Heart Questions
Explore the patterns that emerged as you answered the **Heed Your Heart Questions**.
What wisdom did your Inner Voice impart?

Blissful Activities
Incorporate the **Blissful Activities** that appealed to you into your daily patterns.

Heart Qualities
Review the **Heart Qualities** to determine which ones are qualities that you value.
Use them to become more specific in describing the characteristics you admire in others.

Heart Messages
Analyze the sample messages for clues on how to spotlight the *Intangible Gifts* of others and express your feelings and insights more effectively.

Engage Your Heart
Transform your world and the world of those you care about by sharing your own personalized **Heart Messages**.

Encouragements From the Heart
Refer to the **Encouragements** for a quick summation of the key ideas presented within each chapter.

Follow The Path to Uplifting Hearts.

Wrap your Intangible Gifts in Love and send as many Heart Messages as you can.

They are free.

Acknowledgments

I wish to extend my gratitude to Jeanne Johnson, whose request for advice was the impulse that energized the birth of this book. Her boundless enthusiasm, her encouragement, and her steadfast endorsement of my efforts have carried me along.

I am thankful to Deanna Carney, Jackie Viviano, Kathleen Colley and Barbara Ricotta for the opportunity to expand on their creative inspirations.

To Deahn Boies, I offer an abundance of thankfulness for her soulful intelligence and for the years of conversations we have shared, exploring our complimentary bonds of insights and intuitions.

My deepest appreciation goes to Pete Pilcic for his patience with endless revisions and for his exceptional design sensibility, which brought the content of this book to life.

The cover art of Saundra E. Beretta captures the transformative nature of this book and sets our Uplifted Hearts on the pathway to discovery.

My warmest wishes go to Dr. Shane Kelly for her gentle feedback and content validation and to Norris Van den Berg for his guidance and support in navigating the world of being an author.

The depth, breadth and tenderness of my love go out to my husband, John, who always allows and encourages Me to be Me.

Friends and family will recognize themselves in the **Heart Messages** throughout this book. To them I give my love and admiration for their demonstration of how to enrich the experiences Life has to offer.

You Are So You! **The Path to Uplifting Hearts,** was written with them in mind and comes with the assurance that each message emanates from a cherished place in my heart.

Some of the **Heart Messages** were also influenced by the eloquent words of friends, whose cards and wishes are among my greatest treasures.

Made in the USA
San Bernardino, CA
21 November 2013